Leckie
the education publisher
for Scotland

Higher Psychology

Practise and Pass

FOR SQA EXAMS

Jonathan Firth

ISBN 9780008314590

Published byLeckie & Leckie Ltd
An imprint of HarperCollinsPublishers
Westerhill Road, Bishopbriggs, Glasgow, G64 2QT
T: 0844 576 8126   F: 0844 576 8131
leckieandleckie@harpercollins.co.uk
www.leckieandleckie.co.uk

Commissioning Editor: Kerry Ferguson
Project manager: Alison James

Special thanks to
Louise Robb (copy edit)
Jess White (proofread)
Jouve (layout and illustration)

Printed in Italy by Grafica Veneta S.p.A

A CIP Catalogue record for this book is available from the British Library.

Image credits

P6 (top) © by hafakot/Shutterstock.com; P6 (bottom) © by Respiro/ Shutterstock.com; P7 © by Lane V. Erickson / Shutterstock.com; P9 © by Artur Szczybylo / Shutterstock.com; P10 © by EtiAmmos / Shutterstock.com; P14 © by Diego Cervo / Shuuterstock.com; P16 (top) © by Chinnapong / Shutterstock.com; P16 (bottom) © by RawPixel.com / Shutterstock.com; P18 © by wutzkohphoto / Shutterstock.com; P20 © by Cozine / Shutterstock.com; P28 (top) © by yomogi1 / Shutterstock.com; P28 (bottom) © by arka38 / Shutterstock.com; P29 (top) © by rumruay / Shutterstock.com; P29 (bottom) © by umpapron / Shutterstock.com; P30 © by polumiya / Shutterstock.com; P32 (top) © by Mascha Tace / Shutterstock.com; P32 (middle) © by Meralyx / Shutterstock.com; p32 (bottom) © by solar22 / Shutterstock.com; P33 © by Nitikorn Poonsiri / Shutterstock.com; P34 (top) © by Andrea Danti / Shutterstock.com; P34 (bottom) © by photographee.eu / Shutterstock.com; P35 © by Mrs Opossum / Shutterstock.com; P36 (top) © by agsandrew / Shutterstock.com; P36 (bottom) © by ESB professional / Shutterstock.com; P38 (top) © by Marcos Mesa Sam Wordley / Shutterstock.com; P38 (bottom) © by MonkeyBusiness Images / Shutterstock.com; P39 © by Princeoflove / Shutterstock.com; P42 © by Jess Rodrigues /Shutterstock.com; P43© by Musing Tree Design / Shutterstock.com; P44 © by Rawpixel / Shutterstock.com; P46 © by Minerva Studio / Shutterstock.com; P48 (top) © by Nadia Snopek / Shutterstock.com; P48 (bottom) © by mypokcik / shutterstock.com; P52 © by wan wei / Shutterstock.com; P54 © by Osman. abdelmukarem / Shutterstock.com; P56 © by Shirstok / Shutterstock. com; P58 © by studiolaut / Shutterstock.com; P59 © by igorstevanovic / Shutterstock.com; P64 © by Sangoiri / Shutterstock.com; P66 © by Art Alex / Shutterstock.com; P68 © by Jaroslav Moravcik / Shutterstock. com; P70 © by garagestock / Shutterstock.com; P72 © by roger ashford / Shutterstock.com; P78 © by Daisy Daisy / Shutterstock.com; P79 © by rawpixel.com / Shutterstock.com; P80 © by rawpixel.com / Shutterstock. com; P82 © by Perwara Nicropithak / Shutterstock.com; P88 (top) © by Nat.photo / Shutterstock.com; P88 (bottom) © by Vjacheslav _Kozyrev / Shutterstock.com; P89 © by Hyejin Kang / Shutterstock.com; P90 (top) © by Victor Naumik / Shutterstock.com; P90 (bottom) © by Olga Kuevda / Shutterstock.com; P91 (top) © by Everett Historical / Shutterstock. com; P91 (bottom) © by Everett Historical / Shutterstock.com; P92 (top) © by Lucky Business / Shutterstock.com; P92 (middle) by © makieni / Shutterstock.com; P92 (bottom) © by DGL images / Shutterstock.com; P93 © by Gagliardimages / Shutterstock.com; P94 (top) © by Stuart Monk / Shutterstock.com; P94 (bottom) © by grmarc / Shutterstock.com; P95 © by Sangoiri / Shutterstock.com; P96 (top) © by M-Sur / Shutterstock. com; P96 9bottom) © by mandy Godbehear; Bestphotostudio; Artush / Shutterstock.com; P97 © by Rawpixel.com / Shutterstock.com; P98 (top) © by wavebreakmedia / Shutterstock.com; P98 (bottom) © by Yiorgos GR / Shutterstock.com; P99 © by BlurryMe / Shutterstock.com; P102 (top) © by Evgeny Atamanenko / Shutterstock.com; P102 (bottom) © by pink panda / Shutterstock.com; P104 © by Sunkids / Shutterstock.com; P105 © by CREATISTA / Shutterstock.com; P106 © by Suphaksorn Thongwongboot / Shutterstock.com; P107 © by fizkes / Shutterstock.com; P108 © by fizkes / Shutterstock.com; P109 © by venimo / Shutterstock.com; P110 © by Corepics VOF / Shutterstock.com; P111 © by AshTproductions / Shutterstock.com; P114 © by PHOTOCREO Michael Bednarek / Shutterstock.com; P116 © by Creative Mood / Shutterstock.com; P117 © by Rostislav Stefanek / Shutterstock.com; P118 © by Lorelyn Medina / Shutterstock.com; P120 © by GlOck / Shutterstock.com; P122 © by Aaron Ammat / Shutterstock.com; P123© by Georgejmclittle / Shutterstock.com; P130 (top) © by g-sockstudio / Shutterstock.com; P130 (bottom) © by FS Stock / Shutterstock.com; P132 © by one photo / Shutterstock.com; P133 (top) © by Iakov Filimonov /Shutterstock.com; P133 (bottom) © by Kzenon /Shutterstock.com; P137 © by Ico Maker / Shutterstock.com

All other images © Shutterstock.com or public domain.

Whilst every effort has been made to trace the copyright holders, in cases where this has been unsuccessful, or if any have inadvertently been overlooked, the Publishers would gladly receive any information enabling them to rectify any error or omission at the first opportunity.

Acknowledgements

Firstly, I'd like to thank the team at Leckie and Leckie. They have been very supportive of me as a writer and of psychology as a school and college subject, publishing my first *Leckie Higher Psychology Success Guide* in 2011, followed by the *Leckie National 5 and Higher Psychology Student Book* in 2015, and its second edition in 2018. In particular, I would like to thank Kerry Ferguson, who has overseen every stage of this book.

The style, format and content of the book owe a lot to my interest in the science of memory and learning, about which I have learned from a great many people around the teaching and research communities, in particular my PhD supervisors Professor Ian Rivers and Professor James Boyle. The format is also similar to *Collins AQA GCSE 9-1 Psychology All-in-One Revision and Practice*, a revision guide that I co-wrote for GCSE Psychology, and I would therefore like to acknowledge the work of the editorial team on that project and the support of my co-author Marc Smith.

More broadly, I am deeply grateful for the warmth and support of the many psychology teachers and student teachers that I have worked with in various capacities since I began teaching the subject in 2001. It has been a generous and proactive community to be a part of, from which I have learned a great deal about the subject and about approaches to teaching it. I am certain that some of these ideas have filtered through into the choice of tasks and questions in this book, though any flaws are entirely my own.

Finally, I would like to acknowledge the work of my wife, Fiona Firth, in providing detailed feedback on all stages of this project, and for her unwavering support. When people write books, the contribution of family members tends not to be visible in the final product. It's undoubtedly the case that I couldn't have written this or any of my previous books without her.

Jonathan Firth

CONTENTS

ANSWERS

Check your answers to the Practice Question Book questions and the Practice Test Papers online:
www.leckieandleckie.co.uk/page/Resources

Introduction

This book is designed to support students of Higher Psychology. It can be used either in the classroom, for regular study and homework, or for exam revision.

By combining a revision guide, practice question book, and a full set of practice exam papers, the book includes everything you need to prepare for the Higher Psychology exam.

All topics from the newest (starting in 2018/19) Higher Psychology syllabus are included in the book in full. Sub-topics are presented in easily-absorbed double-page spreads, making it easier to plan your revision. Clear explanations with diagrams and images will help to build long-term memory of new concepts, while quick tests and practice questions help you to check your knowledge and build a deeper understanding as you go along. With an evidence-based guide on how to study as well as advice on exam skills, the book will prepare you for everything you need for the exam, including an ability to recall relevant facts in detail and the skills of in-depth evaluation and analysis.

Using the book

This book is divided into three main sections: a revision guide, practice questions and practice exam papers.

Revision guide

The first section is the revision guide. This summarises the topics from Higher Psychology in a simple way, while retaining the essential information that you need to pass the exam.

There are eight topics covered across the first eight chapters of the revision guide; ensure that you revise the following topics:

- Sleep — mandatory (chapter 1)
- one optional topic from the Individual Behaviour unit — Depression, Memory or Stress (one from chapters 2–4)
- Conformity and Obedience — mandatory (chapter 5)
- one optional topic from the Social Behaviour unit — Prejudice, Social Relationships or Aggression (one from chapters 6–8).

Chapter 9 of the revision guide focuses on applying research across the whole course. The reason for this is that although research is a mandatory element of the Higher Psychology course, there isn't a separate exam section on research (at least, this is the case at the time of writing — always read the most recent SQA documents for your year, and check with your teacher/lecturer if unsure).

Instead, an understanding of research will be tested within the other topics, for example by asking you about ethics in a research study on Sleep, or about the variables studied in an experiment on Conformity. Chapter 9 will help you to develop the skills needed to apply your research understanding in context.

> **! Syllabus note**
>
> Conformity and Obedience make up a single topic. Every Higher Psychology student needs to study the whole of this topic.

Practice questions

The second part of this book contains practice questions based on every topic from Higher Psychology, including all of the mandatory content. Working through these questions will help you to consolidate your knowledge and help prevent forgetting. Memory researchers have shown that answering quizzes and test questions is a more effective way of building memories than re-reading the same information (Roediger & Karpicke, 2006), probably because it provides practice of retrieving information from long-term memory.

The emphasis in this section is to develop and consolidate your knowledge and to identify any gaps or flaws in your understanding, rather than practising exam-style questions. As such, the questions are not necessarily in the same format as those in your final exam, but will probably resemble many of the practice activities that you do in class.

You will find it most effective to attempt the practice questions after a delay of a day or more, rather than immediately after reading the corresponding section of the revision guide. In addition, don't underestimate the value of attempting these questions more than once. If you try them after studying the topic in class, for example, it would be worth answering them again a few weeks later during your exam revision.

Some of the questions in the workbook are in a multiple-choice format or require you to fill in one-word answers. There are also questions that require longer answers. As a guide to how to answer these, consider the various types of questions outlined below.

Direct questions

These questions ask for a simple fact or definition, and don't require any further elaboration. For example, 'During which stage of sleep do dreams mainly occur?' (Answer: REM sleep). You can answer as briefly as you like, as long as you give the correct information.

'Briefly explain' and similar questions

These questions are asking for an accurate written answer without going into depth or detail. Similarly, you might be asked to 'briefly describe' or (less commonly) 'briefly analyse' a concept. As a rough guide, two to three sentences is usually enough.

'Explain' and similar questions

These are similar to the 'briefly' questions described above, except that you are usually expected to give more depth and detail. You should aim to give examples and to back your points up with summarised research evidence where relevant. As a rough guide, a full paragraph is usually expected at the very least, and when tackling such questions in the exam, you should always pay attention to the mark allocation – some may require a short essay. See the Exam Skills chapter later in this section for more information on the skills (evaluate, analyse, etc.) required to answer exam questions successfully.

Summarise research

You won't be asked to 'summarise research evidence' in the Higher Psychology exam, but you may want to briefly summarise a study at the beginning of a longer *analyse* or *evaluate* essay question (see the Exam Skills chapter). It's therefore useful to practise giving summaries of research that are short and to the point, conveying key information without taking too long to write.

The answers to the 'quick tests' from each revision guide section can be found on page 136, and guideline marking instructions and example points for every question in the Practice Question Book are provided for you at **www.leckieandleckie.co.uk/page/Resources**. It's worth noting that for longer question formats in particular there isn't a single 'right' answer, but this feedback will help you work towards the kind of response that will gain a high mark in the exam.

Exam papers

The final section of this book consists of a set of practice exam papers. These follow the style of the final SQA exam and cover all of the course, but they also increase slightly in difficulty from practice exam 1 to practice exam 3, in order to ensure that you are prepared for anything that the exam setters might throw at you. Again, you will need to skip sections on option topics that you haven't done.

Revising for the exam

As is the case for any exam, your revision for Higher Psychology needs to be effective. It should also be efficient, leading to maximum learning in the time available. This chapter provides an evidence-based explanation of how best to revise.

Encoding to memory

If you have studied the option topic of Memory, you already know about some of the many ways that human memory is limited. Information can disappear from our minds really quickly – picture a time when you went to another room and then thought 'what did I come here for … ?'. This is because our working memory has a limited duration and is not responsible for long-term storage. Instead, you need to build an understanding in your long-term memory (LTM) in order to remember it well (see chapter 3 for more on these concepts).

However, working memory does play a key role in learning. Distractions and failing to pay attention can mean that information is lost from working memory, and therefore not learned. It is easiest to focus attention for short spells of time, and when we are not tired or stressed. It is also important to avoid distractions and multi-tasking when studying.

Why we forget

Memories that have been stored in long-term memory can last for decades, but a major problem is that many things that we think we have remembered are either forgotten (if they were not learned effectively) or were never fully memorised in the first place.

New learning needs to be consolidated by regularly retrieving and using the learned information. As an analogy, picture searching for something in your home – a small item that you haven't seen for months. It can be hard to know where to look, and you can find yourself searching around for quite a while. In contrast, if you used the item yesterday, it is (usually) easy to remember where it is. Regular retrieval and practice of what you learn makes it easier to 'find' things in long-term memory.

In effect, this means that learning is not just about taking in information. Instead, retrieving information is essential to building strong, durable memories. So rather than reading your notes and highlighting them, test yourself, and check your understanding – especially after a delay.

Study habits

When you sit down to study, there are numerous ways of making it more effective. The following tips will help ensure that your hard work results in durable long-term memories:

- **Effective note-taking** – use an approach such as the Cornell note-taking system, which organises your page into three sections: one for detailed facts, one for key questions and terms, and the final one for an overview written later (as revision).

- **Elaboration** – this involves making meaningful connections between the to-be-learned concepts and your prior learning, vivid mental images, or applications/uses of a concept. Links to other topics can also be made. A more elaborate idea is more distinctive and well connected to other knowledge, and this makes it easier to remember later on.

- **Concrete examples** – new concepts can be quite vague unless you use examples. Find examples from your textbooks and course notes and note them down or expand on them. You could also make up your own, and have your teacher/lecturer check them.

- **Spacing** – spacing out your study sessions over time leads to information being better remembered, so avoid revising too soon after you first learn something (like on the same day). Also, you should break study sessions into short blocks while still allowing the same overall amount of study time, and return to a topic after a delay rather than doing it all at once.

- **Test yourself using index cards** – as mentioned in the previous chapter, testing yourself is highly effective at improving recall. It is harder to answer a test question than to re-read something, but it's also better for building new memories. The more difficult you find it, the more effective it is. If you can't remember the answer to a question, the act of looking up the answer or correcting your mistakes can also be memorable.

The use of mnemonics

A mnemonic is a memory strategy than can help with recall in an exam situation. Mnemonics don't replace learning, but they help with retrieval of information that might otherwise be easy to forget. As discussed above, repeated retrieval leads to memories being strengthened, so the mnemonic may cease to be necessary after you have used it a few times. A mnemonic is therefore useful at the beginning of the learning process, and for details that are hard to keep straight in your mind.

🔍 **Top tip**

In your revision, use keywords as cues to help avoid forgetting under exam stress.

There are several types of mnemonics:

Type of mnemonic	Example
Acronyms and acrostics – This form of mnemonic involves making words or phrases with the first letters of items you are trying to remember. For example, take several stages of a process and come up with a word that includes all of the initial letters from these stages. Or it may be easier to make up a memorable sentence where the words of the sentences have the same initial letters as the terms you are trying to learn. When it comes to recall, these words or phrases will act as cues, making it easier to remember the terms.	You could use this technique to remember the different factors that affect obedience. First identify each term, forming a list that cuts out any minor words: perceived legitimate authority, socialisation, authoritarian parenting, autonomous/agentic states, proximity, wearing uniform. This provides a set of initial letters ('plasapaaspwu'), and you can then convert these into one or more words (e.g. '*a wasp appals u*'), or a longer phrase.
Visualisation – Visualisation means using a mental image to remember items. The to-be-remembered items have to be converted in some way, for example by associating them with a particular object and locating each object in a place that you can easily visualise, such as your own street. A variation of this technique would be to imagine each object along a journey, such as your route from home to school.	Firstly, associate every key research study that you learn with a particular object, person or creature. Freud's 'little Hans' study could be linked with a horse, and Mori and Arai's (2010) study with a pair of glasses. Each of these objects is then visualised in the location. The stranger the visual image, the better, and it's also good to link the images together – so you could picture an enormous horse wearing glasses, for example.
Stories – Stories are better remembered than other information – psychologists sometimes refer to them as 'psychologically privileged'. This means that information that we learn as a story is better remembered, and you can make use of this effect by inventing stories that link your revision concepts together. You can observe this at work already if you found case studies (little Hans, H.M., etc.) to be easier to remember than other research evidence – this is because they are a form of story about a real person's life. As a mnemonic, you can create a list of key words and use these as the basis of a story (this is sometimes called the 'narrative method').	Terminology will often need to be simplified to form nouns that can feature in a story. For example, for the reorganisational theory of sleep, parasitic and adaptive memories could be simplified to 'parasite' and 'adaptor'. Names like Crick could be altered to similar-sounding verbs or nouns like 'crack'. These are then strung together into the keywords of a sentence, such as 'The enormous parasite cracked the adaptor', and so on into a longer story.

Exam skills

The Higher exam features questions that each follow a single key word, with the most important being:

- **Describe**
- **Explain**
- **Evaluate**
- **Analyse**

In many ways, these are not really questions at all (they don't ask a question like 'What was the method used?') but rather *commands*, telling you what to think about and what to write down. For this reason, the key words at the start of each one are often called **command words**.

The current practice in Higher Psychology is to include only one command word per question. So, for example, you might be asked to 'evaluate x' or 'describe x', but not 'describe and evaluate x'. Note that SQA guidance can change, however, and pay attention to the format of the current specimen question paper on the SQA website.

Key skills – describe and explain

'Describe' questions generally ask you to recall facts, such as the procedure of a research study or the stages of a process. 'Explain' questions require you to show your understanding, which generally involves making links between facts rather than just stating the facts.

Therefore, a question that asks you to *describe* a theory would require you to give information such as who came up with the theory, what it is a theory of, and what the main elements or stages of the theory are. *Explaining* the same theory would require you to show the relationships between these things – what does the theory show, and how do the different parts of it link together? It is also helpful to put in real-world examples when answering explain questions. This helps to show that you understand the concept, and can link it to real-world occurrences of psychological processes.

There are many examples of both of these types of questions in the Practice Questions section of this book.

Key skills – evaluation

Questions that ask you to 'evaluate' a study or theory are typically looking for you to focus on the positive and negative aspects of a study or theory, but to do so in a way that amounts to more than just a list of strengths and weaknesses (for that, you might be asked to 'Briefly explain two strengths and two weaknesses', although such questions are found more at N5 than at Higher level).

The key difference between a list of strengths and weaknesses and a true evaluation is that the latter develops and explains the points made. So, for example, rather than just saying that a study is flawed because it used a small sample of participants, you could explain why a small sample may lead to biased results.

Good evaluation is not just a matter of making a lot of points. Often it will be better to make a smaller number of points, but to go into more detail. Again, long lists of flaws tend to be quite superficial, and evaluation questions require depth and explanation. It is best to develop evaluation as a skill, both because memorisation of lists of strengths and weaknesses often fails to gain credit in the exam, and because learning how to evaluate well is more efficient than trying to memorise sample answers. Developing this skill will help you to evaluate other research and theories that you come across in the future, for example during your future studies or work.

Evaluating a research study

There are four aspects of any study that you can tackle in your evaluation. Some will be more important than others depending on the study, but all could be commented on. The four are outlined below.

Ethics

Here you address any ethical problems such as harm to participants, deception, and so on. Some historical studies in psychology were highly unethical. This is unfortunate for the research participants, but it does give today's psychology students a lot to talk about! Studies that have done a better job of meeting ethical standards can also be evaluated, though. Simply state what features made the study ethical, and what the implications of this might be.

Top tip

Some specific research studies are mandatory in the course, and in other cases, the syllabus instead requires you to learn any study on a particular area (for example, 'the aims, methods, results, evaluation and conclusions of one study into ways of reducing prejudice'). Guidance on this is provided via further Top Tips throughout the Revision Guide.

Methodology

Consider the methodology used in the study. Besides any ethical implications, was the task used quick, efficient, slow, or hard to replicate? Was it unrealistic (i.e. lacking mundane realism) due to being very unlike what people do in everyday life? Did the study maintain internal validity by controlling any extraneous/confounding variables?

One of the easiest things to focus on here is the research method itself. Experiments are controlled and tend to demonstrate clear cause and effect, while other methods – such as natural experiments and correlation studies – generally do not. Surveys and interviews can be criticised on the basis that what people say about their behaviour might be different from what they actually do. For example, people tend to report that they would always help a stranger in need, and say that they would not obey in a Milgram-type experiment – the evidence suggests otherwise!

Sample and population

Consider the sample used. Was it large or small, human or non-human? What age were they, what culture did they come from and was the study conducted a long time ago? All of these issues affect whether findings can be generalised to the broader population in today's society, and therefore can be explained as flaws that result in weaker findings.

Top tip

When discussing the sample used in a study, address the issue of whether the results can be generalised more widely.

In addition, the setting of the study – for example, a lab or a participant's home – can affect how easy it is to generalise from the behaviour studied to real-life situations (i.e. the level of ecological validity can be evaluated).

Impact

At the end of the day, did the study matter? Was it ground-breaking, and did it come up with a new experimental procedure that was then widely used by others? Was it the first to tackle an issue, thus moving science forward, or was it the first to distinguish between two competing theories? These things don't affect the validity of the results, but they can be explained as strengths.

Evaluating a theory

Evaluating a theory is similar in principle to evaluating a research study – you need to comment on and explain strengths and weaknesses, showing how these flaws might affect the validity of the work as a whole. And again, it can be just as good (or better) to fully explain and back up a small number of points, rather than trying to list many strengths/ weaknesses without going into depth.

> **🔍 Top tip**
>
> When evaluating, follow up any factual statements with their implications, such as by stating an ethical weakness and then saying 'this was unethical because …'.

The following series of bullets shows a process that can be followed for most theories.

- Identify a central aspect of the theory, for example the role of rehearsal in Atkinson and Shiffrin's (1968) multi-store model of memory, or the concept of parasitic memories in the reorganisational theory of dreams.

- State that this aspect is good or flawed (it is often easiest to focus on aspects of the theory that are partially or entirely incorrect, or at least disputed).

- Now briefly summarise the evidence relating to your previous statement.

- Now explain why the theory is inconsistent with the evidence. For example, saying: 'If the theory is correct that … then we should observe …. However, the evidence shows that … happens instead. Therefore, this aspect of the theory must be wrong.'

Another way to evaluate a theory is to criticise the body of evidence upon which it is based – thereby making very similar points to those in the previous section. For example, many theories can be criticised for relying too heavily on laboratory studies, or for being based on a research literature that has only studied undergraduates from the USA.

Key skills – analysis

Analysis questions play a large role in the Higher Psychology course. Like evaluation, analysis can be developed as a skill, allowing you to tackle new questions with confidence rather than attempting to memorise sample answers.

Analysis differs from evaluation. Although there is certainly some overlap between the two skills, for example when discussing and elaborating on a strength or weakness, in an 'analysis' question the exam marker will be looking for you to explain points in detail, say why things work in a particular way, and make links with the wider research context.

> **🔍 Top tip**
>
> Start longer answers by setting out the basic facts. When you are answering a longer 'evaluation' question, begin with a paragraph describing the concept/ theory/study before moving on to evaluation. When answering a longer 'analysis' question, begin with a paragraph describing the concept/theory/study and a paragraph on evaluation, before moving on to analysis. This will pick up marks, as can be seen in the practice paper marking instructions.

Often an analytical point will start by stating a fact or detail, but the key thing is to elaborate on that fact, explaining why it was that way and making connections. Such questions allow you to show a deeper understanding – and practising them may also help you to develop that understanding.

Analysing a research study

Analysis of a research study shouldn't be entirely new to you – you have already done this when working on your Assignment (or you will do so soon; see the Guide to the Assignment section that follows this one).

Some of the main ways that you will pick up marks in questions that ask you to analyse a study are as shown in this table.

Top tip

Four of the simplest sources of analysis marks are aims, conclusions, comparisons and applications. Practise identifying these points for all the research you read about.

Source of analysis marks	What to do	Example
Give the aim of the study.	What was the research study actually trying to achieve? How was it advancing knowledge? Explain this, perhaps by stating what was believed at the time the study was carried out.	Czeisler et al. (1990) were aware of the risks and health problems associated with tiredness when working shifts, such as the risk of driving accidents. They therefore wanted to find a fast and effective way to help people modify their circadian rhythms.
Make a methodology point, and then explain it in detail.	Here you identify a particular aspect of the procedures used in the study and explain why researchers made this choice, perhaps explaining the limitations of other options.	Milgram chose the apparatus used in his study because it allowed a clear and objective observation of the level of obedience, which could be expressed in terms of how many buttons a participant had pressed. This made it easy to compare different situational factors in later studies.
Develop an evaluation point.	Follow up on a strength or weakness by explaining the implications of an evaluation you have previously made. Why, for example, is a flaw in the study a problem – what effect does it have on the findings?	Asch's (1951) study used a very artificial task – judging the length of lines, when most real-life situations are more ambiguous. This is a problem because it's hard to know whether the same factors affecting the Asch experiment would affect real-life conformity, such as when people conform to moral or immoral behaviour.

Source of analysis marks	What to do	Example
Make a comparison with a different study.	Here you explain how this study was different from another study, preferably one on the same topic.	In contrast to the classic Asch paradigm, Mori & Arai's (2010) study did not use actors, a feature that they believed led to more authentic responses that were less likely to cause participants to feel suspicious. This makes the findings more valid, and easier to generalise to real life.
Give a conclusion of the study.	Perhaps after briefly stating one or more findings, you give (one of) the conclusions drawn by the researchers.	Dement & Kleitman's (1957) participants were much more likely to report having been dreaming when woken during REM sleep than during non-REM sleep, and so it is clear that REM sleep is the main stage during which people have dreams.
Explain how the study could be applied.	Here you make a link to the real world — most psychology research is connected in some way to real issues, and you can gain credit for explaining a real-world use for the findings.	Although Sherif's (1954) study was conducted on boys at a summer camp, the real-world implications are that any groups that are in conflict could be encouraged to work together through the use of superordinate goals – tasks on which they have to cooperate in order to succeed.

Analysing a theory or concept

Analysing a theory follows a similar principle to analysing a study – you will be explaining points in detail, showing how different aspects connect together, and making links with the wider context. Although theories are all quite different from one another, there are still some general guidelines that you can follow, as shown below.

- A theory might not have an aim, but it does set out to explain something. What? Make this point – why did researchers develop this theory?
- Make a point about the theory and then explain it in more detail.
- Make a broader point after evaluating an aspect of the theory.
- Compare and contrast the theory with another alternative theory (if you know about one).

You might also get the opportunity to analyse the evidence for/against a particular theory. This means explaining one or more research studies that support or go against the theory, and ideally will involve contrasting the findings and explaining why they support or go against the theory. In some situations, it may be possible to refer to evidence supporting one theory as evidence

> 🔍 **Top tip**
>
> You *must* elaborate on analysis points. A short factual sentence is rarely going to be enough to get the mark.

> 🔍 **Top tip**
>
> When tackling an analysis question, ask yourself 'why' for each aspect of a study or theory. For example, why did the researchers use a particular method, why did they choose their sample, why was it considered an improvement on previous research.

against *another* theory. Doing so will show a marker that you are making meaningful links, and beginning to understand the broader context in your topic.

Don't just say that the research supports (or doesn't support) the theory – explain *why* this is the case.

A good analysis answer will make frequent use of words and phrases like:

- 'because'
- 'as'
- 'however'
- 'similarly'
- 'and so'
- 'although'
- 'in contrast to'
- 'this means that' etc.

As well as helping you to link facts with explanations, these words make it easier for an exam marker to identify that your point should be treated as analysis.

Key skills – application and identification

You may also have to 'apply' your knowledge. What this means is using your knowledge in a real-world context. For example, theories of prejudice explain why prejudice occurs, while applications explain how to reduce it.

Questions that relate to application don't always use the command word 'apply' (although this is possible). Instead, you may be asked to describe or explain how something is applied in practice. For example, a question like 'Describe one biological treatment for depression' requires you to explain how treatments for depression are used in the real world. However, the command word 'describe' indicates that you don't need to come up with anything new, you just need to remember and write down factual information about treatments of depression that you have studied.

Another context where you need to apply knowledge is in your Assignment. In the 'Discussion' section, you should explain how your findings could be used in the real world (see the Guide to the Assignment section that follows this one). For example, if you conducted a study on conformity, you could explain how this knowledge could be used in educational programmes to reduce peer pressure.

A small number of exam questions may ask you to 'identify' information. Examples include:

- Identify a flaw in an example study.
- Identify what factor in sleep/conformity/etc. is shown in an example.
- Identify aspects of the results of a study when provided with a table or graph.

These questions are essentially the same as 'briefly describe', and are looking for you to make specific points.

Guide to the Assignment

The Assignment is a mandatory part of Higher Psychology, worth 33% of the overall mark – enough to bring a poor exam mark up to a pass, or even turn a 'C' into an 'A'. It involves planning and running a research project based on the research skills in the course, and writing a scientific lab report that will be submitted to the SQA for marking.

Background reading

In order to fully understand the topic area of your Assignment, you should engage in independent background reading on your topic. Students who have read widely tend to do better in the introduction section of a report. Make use of this textbook, but also dip into other books and sources accessed on the internet. Focus on research articles, as well as blog posts or articles from reputable sources such as universities or the British Psychological Society (the BPS's 'Research Digest' is an excellent source). Google Scholar is a version of the Google search engine that searches specifically for research articles; at this stage in your psychology research career, the 'abstract' or summary of the article will often give you enough information.

It is important that you keep track of your sources. If you come across a useful idea or quote, make sure that you take a note of the source, including publication details. This is good research practice and will save time later when you come to writing up; you will refer to background studies in the text using 'in-line citations' of an author name and year (as you can see throughout this book), and include a references list in a standard format (APA style for references is the one typically used in psychology, though other formats are also acceptable). The following examples show how a journal article and a book would be presented in the references section, using APA style:

- Craik, F. I. M., & Tulving, E. (1975). Depth of processing and the retention of words in episodic memory. *Journal of Experimental Psychology: General, 104*(3), 268–294.
- Milgram, S. (1974). *Obedience to authority*. New York: Harper & Row.

Planning

Once you have read around your research area, you can begin to formulate an aim and hypothesis. The aim states what you are trying to find out, while the hypothesis is a specific prediction of what you expect to find. The experimental hypothesis states that the independent variable (IV) will have an effect on the dependent variable (DV) (the format of the hypothesis and some other aspects of the write-up may differ if you are conducting a non-experimental or correlation study, and you should seek advice from your teacher/lecturer or read the section in the Student Book).

! Syllabus note

The Higher Assignment is worth 40 marks (33%). The guideline word count is 2000–2500 words.

Top tip

This is a brief overview of the Assignment. A more detailed guide, including an example write-up, can be found in Leckie & Leckie's 'National 5 and Higher Psychology Student Book', also by Jonathan Firth.

Top tip

You can plan and conduct the data gathering element of your Assignment in a small group, provided your teacher/lecturer agrees, but the writing and data analysis must all be your own work.

Top tip

Keep detailed notes of your background reading, and make sure you back up all saved files.

For experiments, you will also need to plan whether to use an 'independent groups' or 'repeated measures' design. In some cases, this will be determined by the nature of the study – for some studies such as quasi-experimental comparisons of males and females, it will be necessary to use two separate groups.

Finally, **your planned research must be ethical** (see 'Ethics' in the 'Exam skills' section). An Assignment that violates research ethics in any way will be penalised by the SQA.

🔍 Top tip

The assignment is your own work – you will get guidance, but should not expect your teacher/lecturer to correct your drafts.

Materials

Once you are clear about your aim, you can begin to prepare your materials. If you are using a task sheet, this needs to be drafted out, or you could identify a suitable computer-based experimental task. Information that will be given to participants, such as instructions and debriefing, must also be written out. These tasks can be divided among group members.

You should also decide on whether you are going to do a field or a laboratory experiment. Although you might not have a proper psychology laboratory available to you, you can set up a reasonable substitute by using an empty school room or computer lab, covering any windows and ensuring that you have control over the door to avoid interruptions.

Finally, the way the experiment or study will be run should be planned (and preferably written down) in detail. If more than one person is running the experiment, each should be clear about what they will be doing at any given time. It is advisable to test out all aspects of the procedure before you actually gather data, for example by running a 'pilot' version of the experiment on classmates. As well as highlighting any flaws in the procedure or materials, a pilot study also provides practice in running the experiment, helping researchers come across as well-prepared and professional (Harris, 2002).

Sampling

As you know, there are several different types of sampling (see Research chapter, 'Ethical and scientific standards' section) and random sampling is often considered to be superior, but this is probably beyond the resources available to you as a student. You may only have access to friends, classmates and family, and it is perfectly acceptable to use opportunity sampling, that is, selecting participants on the basis of convenience. However, you should bear in mind the limitations of this technique when you draw your conclusions. Also, remember that for ethical reasons, participants must be at least 16 years of age.

How many participants are required? Unfortunately, there is no definitive answer to this. The greater the number, the stronger your conclusions can be, as a large sample reduces the chances that your results are simply a fluke. As a rough guide, around twelve or more per condition should be enough, bearing in mind that in a repeated measures design the same people participate in more than one condition. One way of increasing the size of your sample would be to combine results with those of other pairs or groups, if their study is being run in exactly the same way.

Allocating participants to conditions

The next stage is to allocate participants to the experimental conditions. This should not be the researcher's choice, as that could lead to experimenter bias. Instead, randomly allocate participants to conditions by tossing a coin, rolling a die, or using a random number generator from the internet.

Analysing the data

You should now use the descriptive statistics you have learned on the Higher course to analyse your data. For an experiment, this will include the mean, median, mode and range, and perhaps the standard deviation as well. Note that all data analysis can and should be done individually – this is not a group task.

Writing up the Assignment

You will now use your background reading and data as the basis of a research report on your findings. Outlined below are some general tips.

- Stick to the scientific facts. Rather than saying 'studies show that …', make reference to specific background research and theories.

- Explain concepts clearly and fully. Don't assume that your reader will know what abbreviations such as REM or LTM stand for – write each term in full the first time you use it.

- Use the passive voice and past tense throughout ('the researcher handed out sheets') – even if you are drafting the report before having completed the study!

- Avoid irrelevant background detail. Background studies in your introduction should be connected to your aim – it's not a general essay about your topic.

The format for the Assignment write-up is as follows:
- Title – expresses the aim of the study in terms of the IV and DV
- Contents page – this should be included as part of your final draft
- Introduction – presents the background, aim and hypotheses
- Method – explains how the study was performed
- Results – shows the results in terms of data and statistical analysis
- Discussion – interprets the results, comments, suggests further research, concludes
- References – directs reader to the sources/books you have mentioned
- Appendices – any materials used (such as task sheets) and raw data analysed are included here

The bulk of the writing – and the available marks – focuses on four main sections: Introduction, Method, Results and Discussion. Each has specific requirements about how it should be written and what it should include.

Introduction

An Introduction in a scientific report is not just a short lead-in to the topic, but one of the longest sections, putting the research in its theoretical context. It is nothing like the introductory section of a discursive essay, but instead has to do three things:

- outline the previous research
- give the aim and rationale for the study
- state the experimental and null hypotheses.

For the Assignment, the research you outline doesn't have to be an exhaustive review, but should show that you understand the key theories behind your work, and should build an argument based on past findings. As a minimum you should include one theory and two research studies, but a strong Introduction will generally include more. For some topics, it will be a good idea to contrast two theories in your Introduction, for example if your experiment aims to find out which of the two theories is more accurate.

You can state the aim either at the beginning or end of the Introduction, but always finish with a formal statement of one or more research hypotheses. These lead on to the rest of the study.

> **🔍 Top tip**
>
> Allocate around 800 words for the Introduction.

Method

The Method section should clearly state what was done in the study and how. It usually has four sub-sections: participants, design, materials/apparatus and procedure (note: actual headings should be used – do not use continuous prose). Four marks are available for ethical issues, so these should be explained in detail and in a way that clearly links to your procedure (don't just state general ethical principles).

- The *participants* sub-section describes who your participants are in terms of their age, sex and background. Sampling (type, and how it was done) should be explained. Do not include information that would make it possible to identify participants, such as their name or school.

- The *design* sub-section states what the research variables were, and (for experiments) whether an independent groups or repeated measures study was used, along with a brief rationale for these choices. Any variables that were kept constant should also be summarised, such as the length of time participants were given to do a task, or where it was done.

- In the *materials* sub-section, you describe any sheets, pictures, videos, apps, etc. that were used. Put copies of these in an appendix, and refer to them in the text with a comment such as 'see Appendix 1'.

- *Procedure* is often the longest sub-section of the four; here you explain exactly how the study was run. Remember to keep it in the passive voice: 'participants were told to …', not 'I told the participants to …'. Although it is tempting to use bullet points, the standard format is to use continuous prose. Mention timings, instructions given and other relevant details. You should also clearly explain how various ethical issues were dealt with (alternatively, this could be done as a separate sub-section).

Results

The Results section includes:

- a statement of how the data were collected
- a brief explanation of how these were analysed (such as percentages, averages or standard deviations)
- a justification of the choice of analysis
- a table showing all mean scores and other descriptive statistics (not 'raw' data – that goes in an appendix)
- one or more graphs highlighting key findings from the results
- comments summarising the main findings
- a statement of the main findings in terms of the experimental hypothesis.

> ### 🔍 Top tip
> When including a graph or table, give it a title, and refer to it in the text ('Figure 1, above, shows …'). Label the axes of a graph.

> ### 🔍 Top tip
> Don't forget to say clearly whether the results support the hypothesis or not, but don't go into an explanation at this point – that belongs in the Discussion section.

Discussion

The Discussion section analyses the findings, and evaluates and comments on the study as a whole.

First, a brief statement of the main findings should be given, and these must then be interpreted in terms of the hypotheses. This will involve a bit of repetition from the Results section, but it makes the Discussion easier to follow, and you can also go into more detail here, considering explanations of each finding and commenting on smaller aspects of the data.

The section will then analyse the results and attempt to explain them in terms of the theories and studies covered during the Introduction section. There are a lot of marks for this, so give it plenty of space and attention.

Analysing your own study involves exactly the same skill as analysing any other study that you have read about in Psychology. If you can't remember how to do this, refer back to the 'Exam skills' section of this book.

Next, you will evaluate your work. Again, this involves the same skill of evaluation that you have been learning about throughout the course. Some of the key things that you should comment on include:

- ethical flaws
- flaws with the sample, such as it being too small or non-random
- flaws with the running of the study
- any other reasons why the results might have been unclear or biased.

It is not enough just to list flaws (and strengths) – you also need to comment on them, and suggest how you could improve them in future studies.

Another inclusion in this section is a 'big picture' comment on what future research could be done to expand on your work, and how the study's findings could be applied in the real world.

Finally, you give a brief conclusion – a short summary (1–2 sentences) of the main finding in terms of the aim and hypothesis.

> ### 🔍 Top tip
> Allocate around 800 words for the Discussion.

References and appendices

As noted earlier, your write-up should include a References section, with a list of every source you have used in a standard format. There should be a one-to-one correspondence between citations made during the introduction or other sections, and the sources listed in the References section. APA is the standard format used throughout psychology research worldwide, and in many other subjects. You can access APA style via Google Scholar, or use the examples in this and other psychology textbooks.

Appendices are not a section as such, but rather a set of supplementary material that appear at the back of your write-up. Each appendix should be labelled (for example, 'Appendix 1', 'Appendix 2' and so on). Every one should be referred to at some point in the main text.

You might include the following types of items as appendices.

- Materials used for the experiment, such as task sheets and questionnaires. These are too long to put in the Method section, so they go in an appendix instead.

- Consent forms, participant information sheet, instructions, debriefing statements, etc. You should only include a blank example consent form, not a completed one.

- Raw data and calculations. This means the individual scores from each participant; the Results section should only have summarised data (e.g. the mean) and the same goes for graphs. Note that including raw data and calculations allows your marker to check your arithmetic, and failing to do so will lose you marks.

> ## 🔍 Top tip
>
> In the appendices, as in the Results section, any participant data must be anonymised. You **must not** include participant or school names, or any other information that would allow individuals to be identified.

If you used slides from presentation software for instructions, or for a task, these should be included. They can be small (e.g. nine slides printed onto a single page), but it must be possible for a marker to read any text.

If you used an online experiment, then give the URL for the relevant website, and it would also be useful to include one or more screenshots.

Troubleshooting ethical issues in your Assignment

Many assignment ideas have potential ethical flaws, and these are not always apparent to candidates who have not yet studied research ethics in any depth.

The following table highlights some common problems, and gives advice about how to avoid them.

Planning issue	Ethical flaw	Possible solution(s)
Our planned study will be carried out on S5 school pupils in November/December.	Many S5 pupils will be under the age of 16 in the autumn, and therefore too young to take part in your assignment.	In schools, data gathering could be carried out on S6s only. In other settings, ensure that anyone who takes part is actually 16 by asking for volunteers of that age or over, or by asking them to state their age on the consent form and making it very clear that they have to be 16+.
We are doing an Asch-type study, where a group of participants will be asked to guess the length of lines, and some of the research team will give fake answers.	Studies should not feature deception or stress to participants, and the Asch study included both of those things. Replications of the Jenness study would also be problematic due to the stress of the group situation.	Generally, you are advised to steer clear of conformity experiments. If you do wish to focus on the topic, you could conduct a survey using a questionnaire with conformity scenarios/vignettes rather than putting people in real situations. This method has its limitations but avoids the major ethical flaws.
The study will involve a member of the research team pretending to collapse/drop a pile of books/etc.	Such studies tend to involve passers by who have not consented to take part, may be under the age of 16, and may feel stressed by the event.	Don't use any design which involves covert observation of people who have not consented to take part! As well as the ethical flaws, assignments should be based on a Higher topic, and this relates more to the N5 topic of Altruism.
The study will involve giving caffeine/energy drinks to participants and then measuring the effect on their sleep.	This could sleep deprive or otherwise harm participants, potentially putting them in danger (e.g. if driving) or affecting their school work. A similar issue applies to plans involving extra screen time, alcohol, or waking participants up during the night.	Rather than interfering with participants' sleep, use a questionnaire to ask them about the sleep habits and consumption of caffeinated drinks/use of screens. This can obtain similar information without stressing or harming participants, as it focuses on behaviour which is happening anyway. Better still, you can give them information about good 'sleep hygiene' as part of your debrief.

Planning issue	Ethical flaw	Possible solution(s)
Our study involves a memory experiment where video clips of car crashes will be shown to participants and they will then be misled about these, as was done by Loftus and colleagues.	Watching a car crash could be distressing for some participants, for example if they or a loved one has recently been involved in an accident. There is also an element of deception in this plan.	A similar aim could be achieved by showing less traumatic videos, such as a clip of a sports match. Rather than misleading participants about these, some participants could be given extra information (e.g. the context/background) and others not, or forgetting based on cultural/schema knowledge (sports fans v's non-sports fans) could be compared.
Our study will give participants an impossible puzzle – a jigsaw with one piece missing – and then measure their performance under a time limit in order to measure stress.	This situation will deliberately stress participants. It's difficult to judge in advance how stressed some participants might feel, and it's possible that some might be very upset and/or experience health problems as a result.	A safer and also more ecologically valid choice would be to measure stress levels in a real study situation, such as when doing their homework. Alternatively, stress could be investigated using questionnaire research about daily hassles and uplifts.
We plan to survey people by going out to the High Street and asking them to take part in our study.	It's possible that approaching members of the public could put you at risk.	The same questionnaire could be put online and distributed to friends and family members, asking participants to declare that they are 16+ before consenting.
We want to interview the pupils in our class who are from ethnic minorities, to find out what it is like to be discriminated against.	Being singled out as research participants in this way on the basis of their race or nationality may be upsetting for classmates.	Use a procedure that could apply to all members of a class who you are using as your sample, for example a more generic questionnaire about prejudice and discrimination.
We want to do a study on depression which looks for signs of major depression and dysthymia by asking classmates about their mental health.	Even if other ethical standards are met (informed consent, confidentiality of data, no participant names in the report, etc), this is a sensitive matter, and very intrusive.	Do not use questionnaires which ask for sensitive information such as participants' mental health, worries, finances, sexual habits, etc. A safer option, still linking to the depression topic, would be a questionnaire about people's beliefs about depression, which could be used to see whether perceptions of the disorder are accurate or not.

Always check with a teacher or lecturer, and if you are in two minds about whether something would be ethical or not, it's probably best not to proceed with that idea.

Part 1: Revision Guide

Sleep and dreams

1 Sleep and dreams

The biology of sleep

Circadian rhythms

Circadian rhythms are the body's natural processes that vary over a 24-hour cycle. One example of a circadian rhythm is the sleep-wake cycle. This biologically controlled process ensures that we are awake and asleep at roughly the same times each day and night.

The area of the brain that controls our circadian rhythms is the **hypothalamus**, and in particular a part of the hypothalamus called the **suprachiasmatic nucleus (SCN)**. The SCN gets information about light levels from nerve cells in the eyes, informing the brain when it is time to sleep.

The SCN controls **melatonin**, a hormone that makes us feel sleepy.

- Melatonin is released into the bloodstream when it starts to get dark.
- Melatonin makes a person feel drowsy, and eventually fall asleep.
- Melatonin levels peak in the middle of the night and then decrease towards daytime.
- Melatonin supplements are sometimes given to children or adults with sleep problems.

! Syllabus note

This topic is mandatory for all Higher Psychology students.

awakening

happy

sleep

suprachiasmatic nucleus (body clock)

Adenosine

Another chemical that affects sleep is **adenosine.** Adenosine builds up in our neurons during the day. This also causes us to feel gradually more tired as the day goes on. When we sleep, this build-up is cleared, and the adenosine in cells gets replaced by energy.

The effects of adenosine help to explain the way caffeine can interfere with sleep. Caffeine blocks adenosine receptors in neurons, making the body less responsive to the build-up of adenosine and reducing feelings of tiredness (see the final section of this chapter).

Sleep stages

There are multiple **stages** during a night's sleep, each of which occurs more than once. The final stage is called **REM sleep**, and the other sleep stages are sometimes collectively called **non-REM sleep**:

Stage1
light sleep

REM Stage
breathing becomes more rapid and irregular

Stage2
waves slow down

Sleep Cycle

Stage4
no eye movement or muscle activity

Stage3
delta waves begin to appear

Stage	Feature	Approximate duration
Stage 1	Drifting off/easily woken	10 minutes
Stage 2	Sleeping soundly/sleep spindles occur	15 minutes
Stage 3	Electroencephalogram (EEG) brain monitor begins to show some delta waves/very unresponsive to the environment	20 minutes
Stage 4	Groggy and disorientated if woken	45 minutes
REM sleep	REM; body paralysed; dreams occur	25 minutes

📖 Dement and Kleitman's (1957) study of REM sleep

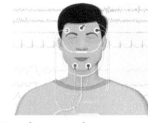

Aim: Dement and Kleitman aimed to understand the function of REM sleep, and whether eye movements were connected to the content of dreams.

Method: Nine adults (seven male, two female) came to a sleep laboratory for a polysomnography, having avoided alcohol and caffeine during the day. They were woken several times during the night by the researchers and asked if they had been dreaming, and if so, what their dream had been about and how long it had lasted.

Findings: The participants said that they had been dreaming if woken during REM sleep on almost 80% of wakings, compared to around 9% if woken during non-REM sleep. They also said that their dream had been shorter if they were woken 5 minutes after the start of REM sleep, compared to being woken 15 minutes after it started. Eye movements did appear to link to what participants had been dreaming about.

Evaluation: This study used a small sample, and its artificial setting may have affected the quality of sleep or the content of dreams. Evidence that REM sleep is dream sleep has been supported by subsequent research, but the findings linking dream content to eye movements have not. The study focused on adults, so the results can't be generalised to children.

Zeitgebers

As mentioned, the SCN releases melatonin when it gets dark. However, to an extent the SCN can keep track of time without external cues. Its own internal or 'endogenous' cues to the sleep-wake cycle are the reason that we maintain a 24-hour schedule of sleep even when travelling to countries with different time zones.

> ## 🔍 Top tip
>
> A polysomnography is a study that uses multiple measures of brain and bodily processes during sleep. It uses an EEG to measure brain waves across the different sleep stages.

Zeitgeber is another name for external (also called 'exogenous') cues. When we are exposed to normal conditions, the brain avoids gradually shifting its circadian rhythm forward or back because of zeitgebers – a term that literally means 'time givers' (in German). Light and darkness are particularly important zeitgebers, telling our brain that it is time to sleep or wake up.

In our evolutionary past, we would start to feel sleepy as it got darker. Now we use artificial lights and stay awake when it is dark outside. Researchers have found that this can disturb our circadian rhythms and affect the quality of later sleep.

The SCN's endogenous cues mean that we could, in principle, stay in total darkness for a long period of time and maintain an approximately 24-hour bodily cycle, releasing melatonin once a day. This was put to the test by French researcher Michel Siffre, who slept in a cave in perpetual darkness for several weeks. In a test monitored by NASA, it was found that his circadian rhythms maintained a cycle of just over 24 hours. His sleep-wake cycle shifted forward by just a few minutes daily. It can be concluded that the brain is able to maintain an approximately 24-hour cycle due to endogenous cues, but it requires external cues to maintain the body clock more precisely.

Individual differences in circadian rhythms

People often describe themselves as 'not a morning person', and there are genuine individual differences in the biology of people's circadian rhythms:

- Some people are more prone to early waking than others. Sleep researchers call this group 'larks'.

- Others tend to get up late and stay up late. Researchers nickname this group 'owls' or 'night owls'.

- Differences are largely genetic, meaning that people maintain similar habits and preferences throughout life, and cannot choose to be a lark or an owl.

- Only around 25% of people are true night owls.

The technical name for this is your **chronotype**, and it can affect functioning. Owls tend to do better at logical tasks in the evening and creative tasks in the morning, while the majority of people are the opposite.

As society is largely set up to suit larks, owls can be at a disadvantage in the workplace, sports, and other areas of life, and even tend to get worse grades (as exams are not usually held in the evening).

There are also variations in terms of how much sleep people need.

- Most adults need around 7–8 hours sleep per night to function well.

- Babies and young children need more sleep, with newborns sleeping for the majority of the time but in shorter spells and less deeply.

- The amount of sleep needed reduces through the lifespan, with the lowest levels in old age.

- A few people can function well on six hours of sleep or less, but most people who get a small amount of sleep are accumulating a sleep debt, that is, a lack of sleep that they need to 'pay back' later.

- In adolescence, the body clock shifts gradually later until the mid-to-late teens, and then starts to get earlier again.

In a study of over 3000 teenagers, Wolfson and Carskadon (1998) found that students who regularly got more sleep obtained higher grades, suggesting that we need a full night's sleep to consolidate new learning. The mean amount of sleep reported among their sample of 13 to 17 year olds was seven hours and 20 minutes, and they argued that most adolescents need more than this. However, the study did not follow participants longitudinally so cannot draw conclusions about the long-term effects of poor sleep.

As we have seen, the brain is involved in sleep in several ways.

- The SCN controls our body clock and triggers the release of melatonin.
- Adenosine builds up in our neurons as a natural by-product of the brain's daily activities, leading to fatigue later in the day.
- The brain cycles through REM and several non-REM sleep stages during the night, each with their own characteristic electrical activity in the brain.
- Sleep is important for the brain to stay in good health, and to consolidate memories.

Key concepts

- Circadian rhythms
- Hypothalamus
- The suprachiasmatic nucleus (SCN)
- Melatonin
- Adenosine
- Sleep stages
- REM sleep
- Non-REM sleep
- Zeitgebers
- Chronotype

Quick test

1. What term is given to the body's 24-hour rhythms such as the sleep-wake cycle?
2. According to Dement and Kleitman, what happens during REM sleep?
3. What part of the brain contains the suprachiasmatic nucleus (SCN)?
4. What chemical builds up in our brain cells during the day?

The restoration theory of sleep

Oswald's (1966) **restoration theory** of sleep states that the main function of sleep is to allow the body and the brain to carry out repair tasks, such as:

- repairing minor bodily injuries
- removal of waste chemicals in the muscles
- replenishing neurotransmitters and/or energy in the brain.

The rationale is that inactivity makes restoration possible because no damage is being done to body tissues, or because toxins/waste production is reduced.

Shapiro et al. (1981) studied runners and found that non-REM sleep rose from 25% to 45% of total sleep over the next two nights. This supports the idea that the body is using sleep time to repair minor damage.

> **Top tip**
>
> Put these restoration functions on an index card for revision.

Body, or brain?

It is important to distinguish between **bodily restoration** and **brain restoration**. Hobson (2005) believed that sleep is entirely for the brain.

Horne and Harley (1988) believed that the longer sleep in the Shapiro study (see above) was caused by a warming of the brain. To test this, they heated people's heads using a hairdryer, and four of their six participants were found to have a longer period of non-REM sleep. This finding contradicts the idea that sleep repairs the body.

Adam and Oswald (1983) believed that the brain and body are restored in different sleep stages:

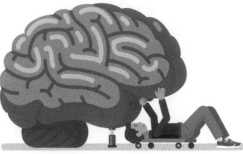

- REM sleep allows the growth and reparation of neurons and replenishment of neurotransmitters
- slow-wave sleep is essential for bodily restoration.

Their evidence included the following findings.

- People who have had spinal operations or have taken drug overdoses have longer periods of REM sleep, supporting the idea that this stage is essential for repairing the brain and other parts of the nervous system.
- The level of neurotransmitters in the brain reduces during the day, indicating that it needs to be replenished at night.

> **Top tip**
>
> Adam and Oswald (1983) argued that REM sleep is for brain restoration, while non-REM sleep is for bodily restoration.

Analysis and Evaluation

Restoration is not the only possible explanation for why all animals sleep. Researchers agree that sleep must have been useful to animals throughout our evolution, but it's possible that rather than restoring the body, sleep was important for saving energy, or to reduce the threat of danger that would occur if a creature was wandering around at night. However, these ideas don't explain that we sleep more when the body needs to repair. Overall, it seems safe to say that restoration is one purpose of sleep, but it might not be its only purpose.

Another piece of evidence from animals is that carnivores sleep much more than herbivores. Assuming that all creatures need to restore injuries to a similar extent, this difference is hard to explain in terms of restoration, and suggests that sleep plays an important role in conserving energy when a creature is not feeding.

Restoration also struggles to explain why animals lose consciousness during sleep. This is not an evolutionary advantage, and repairs to the body could potentially be achieved through simply resting. Brain restoration, on the other hand, might only be possible if the brain is 'switched off' during the process.

Sleep deprivation in humans results in poorer performance and an increased chance of accidents. This supports the restoration theory, although these findings also indicate brain rather than bodily restoration; body function appears to be more or less normal after sleep deprivation – short-term sleep deprivation doesn't make people ill or worse at sports.

Sleep probably has multiple functions. Another key function that takes place during sleep is the processing of information and consolidation of new memories. It also seems likely that REM sleep and non-REM sleep have different functions from each other. It is therefore probably over-simplistic to suggest that sleep is just about restoration.

It is unclear whether the increased REM sleep after brain injury is due to restoration. Key processes such as consolidating memories may take longer if the brain has been injured, increasing the length of this stage.

Quick test

1. Name three key repair processes that could occur during sleep.
2. What did Horne and Harley (1988) find when they heated participants' heads with a hairdryer?
3. How did Adam and Oswald (1983) divide up the possible restoration functions of REM sleep and non-REM sleep?

Key concepts

- Restoration theory
- Bodily restoration
- Brain restoration

Biological and psychoanalytic explanations of dreaming

Biological explanation of dreams

As with other aspects of sleep, the processes that occur when we have dreams can be explained biologically. As we have seen, dreaming occurs in the REM sleep stage. Biological psychologists think that dreams largely result as a side effect of brain activity during sleep, and are therefore meaningless. This contrasts greatly with Freud's ideas (see below).

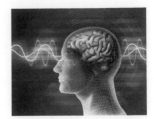

The **activation-synthesis hypothesis** states that dreams result from random firing of neurons.

- Neurons in a brain area called the **pons** become active.
- These send messages to the **neocortex** – the outer area of the brain, which processes thoughts and memories.
- The neocortex tries to make sense of the messages, making up stories that form dreams.

The 'activation' refers to the firing of neurons in the pons, while 'synthesis' refers to the neocortex turning ideas into a dream that makes sense.

Evaluation

The biological explanation of dreams fits with scientific evidence about the activity of different areas of the brain during sleep. However, it doesn't entirely explain why some people have recurring dreams.

This idea also struggles to explain why most dreams make sense to the dreamer, and that experiences from the previous day tend to appear during dreams (Domhoff, 2005).

Psychoanalytic explanation of dreams

Psychoanalytic (or 'psychodynamic') psychology is a historical approach that was very influential in the study of dreams. Researcher Sigmund Freud believed that dreams involve wish fulfilment (Freud, 1900).

Psychoanalysts believe that there are different parts to the mind, and that only some thoughts are accessible. The conscious mind – the 'ego' – contains thoughts that we are aware of, such as our rational beliefs about the world. Other thoughts are entirely unconscious, meaning that they are inaccessible – they affect our behaviour, but we don't know about them. This part of the mind is called the 'id', according to the approach.

There are some thoughts that can become conscious if we make the effort, and these are known as our preconscious thoughts. Essentially, the **preconscious** is an area of the mind on the border between the ego and the id. Memories of our dreams are in the preconscious, meaning that they are not easy to access, but it is possible for us to do so.

Two important terms to be aware of are the manifest content and the latent content of dreams.

- The **manifest content** is what the dream appears to be about.
- The **latent content** is what (according to the psychoanalytic approach) the dream is really about.

Understanding a dream involves analysis of the manifest content in order to reveal the latent content.

The psychoanalytic approach is known for the case study method (see the Research chapter). Freud conducted a case study of 'little Hans', a boy who had a phobia of horses.

Hans had several dreams that Freud studied, including a dream that he was married to his own mother (Freud, 1909). Freud believed that Hans' dreams indicated wish fulfilment – they showed his unconscious desire to be a grown man.

Role of defence mechanisms

Psychoanalytic **defence mechanisms** (such as regression, denial and displacement) can be seen in this theory.

- Repression involves putting unwanted thoughts from the conscious 'ego' into the unconscious 'id'. Repressed desires return during dreams.

- Displacement may occur within the dream. This is where something unimportant is brought to prominence, in order to shift attention away from what is really important.

- **Secondary elaboration** is where a dream is distorted by the dreamer's own interpretation, or things that they later add when thinking about the dream.

Dream symbols themselves can be seen as a form of defence mechanism. We dream in symbols, according to this approach, because this cloaks the true meaning of our dream, thus making it less threatening.

Evaluation

The psychoanalytic approach moved the study of dreams forward (previously, people believed that dreams predicted the future), and had a major cultural impact. However, the science behind it is deeply flawed for the following reasons.

- Freud relied heavily on case studies, which are hard to generalise to other people.

- Psychoanalysts do not all agree on how to interpret dreams; Jung (1964) disagreed with Freud's methods.

- The approach struggles to give a satisfactory explanation of nightmares.

- It has never been reliably established that there is an 'id' or unconscious which works the way that Freud believed.

> ### 🔍 Top tip
>
> A more detailed explanation of psychological approaches can be found in Leckie & Leckie's 'National 5 and Higher Psychology Student Book', also by Jonathan Firth. This includes descriptions of brain areas relevant to the biological approach, and an explanation of the theories behind the psychoanalytic approach.

> ### 🔑 Key concepts
>
> - Activation-synthesis hypothesis
> - Pons
> - Neocortex
> - Psychoanalytic/ psychodynamic explanations
> - Preconscious
> - Latent content
> - Manifest content
> - Secondary elaboration
> - Defence mechanisms

> ### Quick test
>
> 1. What is the term for the biological theory that dreams are due to random firing of neurons in the pons?
> 2. What is the key characteristic of the psychoanalytic approach to dreams?
> 3. Which term means the true meaning of dreams according to Freud's theory?

Cognitive processes in sleep and dreams

The cognitive approach states that the purpose of sleep is to facilitate our cognition (thinking), for example by organising memories.

One key idea is that sleep facilitates **information processing**. According to this view, switching off for a night's sleep allows new information to be sorted, stored and consolidated. Supporting evidence behind this idea includes:

- Mednick et al. (2003) found that learning could be consolidated by a nap
- Mazza et al. (2016) found that splitting study sessions over two days with a night's sleep in between reduced the practice time needed by half.

Sleep may even help with creativity and **problem solving**. Sometimes, it appears that solutions or creative ideas occur after a delay when a person is not thinking about a task – an idea known as **incubation**.

- Rasch & Born (2013) found that people who napped woke up in a 'hyperassociative' phase, which led to an openness to associations.

- Larks are more creative in the evening, while owls are more creative in the morning.

Reorganisation theory

A cognitive theory of dreaming is the **reorganisation theory** (Crick & Mitchison, 1986). It is based on **reverse learning**, meaning that learning can be undone during REM sleep. Crick and Mitchison proposed two categories of memories:

- **adaptive memories** – useful memories
- **parasitic memories** – harmful memories that lead to obsessions and compulsive behaviour.

They believed that the cortex can become overloaded, and parasitic memories are deleted during sleep to make space. As random memories are activated, dreams are produced.

An alternative view from Domhoff (2005) focuses on the subjective meaning of the dreams. He believes a dream is what happens when the mind does not have another task to engage in, and they reflect our knowledge and culture. Because of this, dreams often reflect what we have been thinking about during the day. This is known as the **continuity hypothesis** of dreaming.

Research evidence

Craik and Mitchison argued that reverse learning during REM sleep allows the brain to be smaller and more efficient. They supported this claim by referring to large-brained species that lack REM sleep – the echidna and two species of dolphin.

They also ran neural network computer models of learning, finding that the storage of such systems is easily overloaded and that reverse learning could address this problem. The models acted in random and repetitive ways, which the researchers compared to human obsessions and hallucinations.

Evaluation

There are a lot of flaws with Crick and Mitchison's reorganisation theory.

- The theory is based on animal and computer models of memory.
- People don't seem to forget memories via sleep, even if they try to do so.

- Patients with post-traumatic stress disorder (PTSD) often suffer repetitive nightmares, suggesting that sleep does not delete harmful memories.
- Human long-term memory has an unlimited storage capacity, which counters the idea that it is necessary to delete memories.

🔍 Top tip

Running computer simulations of thought processes is a typical method used as part of the cognitive approach to psychology.

A strength of the reorganisational theory is that it's clear about why REM sleep could be important – its purpose is to make our cognitive processes more efficient. The theory is also consistent with some of the biological evidence, such as the activation-synthesis theory.

Overall, the reorganisation theory in its original form does not have much support nowadays, but the broader idea that sleep is *important* for cognitive abilities such as memory and problem solving is more widely accepted. Nowadays, researchers increasingly agree that sleep is essential to strengthen and consolidate memories, rather than to delete them.

The continuity hypothesis helps to explain cultural differences in dreams; Domhoff notes that hunter-gatherer cultures dream more about animals than do people in industrialised countries.

🔑 Key concepts

- Information processing
- Problem solving
- Incubation
- Reorganisation theory
- Reverse learning
- Parasitic memories
- Adaptive memories
- Continuity hypothesis

Quick test

1. Why are parasitic memories deleted, according to Crick and Mitchison?
2. What computer-based evidence was given in support of the reorganisational theory?
3. Do other researchers agree that sleep causes forgetting?

Factors that affect sleep quality

Drugs

Caffeine is a stimulant drug. It blocks adenosine receptors, affecting the natural tendency to become fatigued during the day. Caffeine can be obtained in multiple ways, including:

- drinks such as coffee, tea, or some types of fizzy juice
- foods such as chocolate.

It takes over five hours for the level of caffeine in the blood to drop by half, meaning that it can affect sleep later in the day.

Other stimulant drugs (legal or otherwise) that affect sleep include nicotine, cocaine and amphetamines. All of these enter the bloodstream and directly affect brain function.

Certain drugs can cause drowsiness; these include illegal drugs and prescription drugs. One example is anti-histamine, an over-the-counter medication often used for allergies.

Alcohol can also cause some drowsiness, although the body quickly develops a tolerance to its effects, and it can lead to more frequent wakings.

Light

Artificial light from lightbulbs or screens acts as a zeitgeber, inhibiting the SCN from releasing melatonin when we want to sleep. The light from low-energy lightbulbs and from phone or computer screens contains a large proportion of blue wavelengths, which have a stronger effect on melatonin than other wavelengths of light.

Chang et al. (2015) studied the bedtime use of light-emitting eReaders. Their participants released less melatonin, took longer to get to sleep, had less REM sleep, and were less alert in the morning. This suggests that it can be highly problematic to look at screens in the hour or so before bedtime, and that even people who don't suffer from insomnia could be experiencing poorer sleep quality.

Shift work and jet lag

Shift work can also affect sleep. During a night shift the person's circadian rhythms are telling the body to sleep, but they need to stay awake. Then, during the day, they may find it hard to sleep soundly.

Jet lag can cause a similar problem. When people travel to a different time zone by plane, they may feel sleepy during the day (hypersomnia) and wakeful at night (insomnia). This is because the SCN still releases melatonin when it is evening in the old time zone, due to the body's endogenous cues.

Aim: This study aimed to test whether bright light exposure would help nightshift workers fully adapt to daytime sleeping. Previous research had shown that the presence of light or darkness can 'reset' the suprachiasmatic nucleus by up to 12 hours.

Method: Eight men came to the researcher's lab for 'nightshifts' on six consecutive evenings. They had to stay awake, do cognitive tests, and report on their own alertness and mood. The experimental group were exposed to very bright light during the nightshift, while the control group experienced normal artificial lighting.

Findings: Measures of hormones and body temperature showed that circadian rhythms shifted by over 9 hours among the experimental group, while the control group stayed roughly the same. Alertness and performance on cognitive tests were also affected.

Evaluation: A strength was that multiple biological measures were taken, and the difference between the mean low-point of body temperature of the control versus the experimental group was huge, and statistically unlikely to have occurred by chance. The small all-male sample made it harder to generalise the results. Extraneous variables such as diet were not fully controlled.

Impact of factors that affect sleep

Lifestyle factors such as light and drugs can lead to **insomnia** – an inability to get to sleep or stay asleep. This may lead to a knock-on effect of extreme sleepiness the following day. Excessive sleepiness is known as **hypersomnia**.

Reduced sleep can be harmful in numerous ways.

- It can put people in a bad mood, and over the longer term it harms mental health, making people more prone to depression.
- It affects daytime functioning, slowing reaction times and affecting working memory.
- Over the long term, it can contribute to problems with physical health, such as coronary heart disease, digestive illnesses, and reproductive problems (Czeisler et al., 1990).

Insomnia is often treated using sedative sleeping pills, but they are not recommended for long-term use, and they fail to tackle the causes of poor sleep.

🔍 **Top tip**

The Dement and Kleitman (1959) and Czeisler et al. (1990) studies are mandatory for Higher students, and you must therefore learn them in detail.

🔑 **Key concepts**

- Light
- Drugs
- Shift work
- Jet lag
- Insomnia
- Hypersomnia

Quick test

1. Why can looking at a screen before bed be problematic?
2. Name one mental or physical problem that can result from poor sleep.

Depression

2   Depression

What is depression?

! Syllabus note

This topic is in the Individual Behaviour unit. Higher Psychology students must study Depression <u>or</u> Memory <u>or</u> Stress.

Depression is part of a broader area known as psychopathology – the study of mental illness. It relates to a severely low, unhappy mood and a loss of interest or pleasure in one's usual activities. A depressed mood can also indicate other psychological disorders. Mild depression does not always indicate a disorder.

Defining psychological disorders

It is difficult to define which thoughts, feelings or behaviours are **normal** and which are **abnormal** as it depends on a subjective point of view, and also on social norms that change over time and between cultures.

Where possible, psychologists avoid basing diagnosis on their personal opinion and instead try to use objective ways of defining what is normal and what is not. Two in particular are based on **harm** and **distress**.

- Is the behaviour or feeling causing the individual distress?
- Is the behaviour or feeling harming the individual?

A broader view of harm includes anything that prevents a normal life. This could include being able to keep yourself clean and fed, having positive relationships, or being able to concentrate on tasks. The degree or frequency of a harmful behaviour is important in determining the severity of a behaviour.

The DSM-5

'DSM' stands for 'diagnostic and statistical manual' and the current version is the 5th edition, and is therefore called **DSM-5**. It helps psychiatrists and clinical psychologists diagnose people with disorders such as depression and phobias. The DSM-5 lists 271 different psychological disorders, categorised into groups such as mood disorders, eating disorders or sleep disorders. The manual uses lists of symptoms and defines whether someone has a disorder in terms of how many symptoms they show and for how long.

These criteria help to make diagnosis less subjective. However, it has been criticised for 'medicalising' normal experiences such as grief and anxiety.

Characteristics of major depressive disorder

Major depressive disorder (or 'major depression') is a mood disorder described in the DSM-5. To be diagnosed, individuals must show at least one of the two key symptoms – low mood, or loss of interest in one's usual activities – on a daily basis for at least two weeks, as well as at least four other symptoms from the following list (and therefore 5+ symptoms in total):

- difficulties in sleeping
- lack of energy/lethargic or agitated

- change in body weight
- feelings of worthlessness and guilt
- difficulty in concentrating
- thoughts of death or suicide.

Major depression has a massive impact on public health and wellbeing. 20–30% of people have at least one episode of major depression during their lifetime. A percentage of the most severely depressed individuals commit suicide, making it one of the most dangerous psychological problems.

🔍 Top tip

One occurrence of a disorder is called an 'episode'.

Characteristics of persistent depressive disorder

Persistent depressive disorder (PDD; also called 'dysthymia') is another disorder described in DSM-5. The key difference between PDD and major depression is its duration and severity. A patient could be diagnosed with PDD with just three of the symptoms above (rather than the five for a diagnosis of major depression), but must show them for two years or more.

Characteristics of bipolar mood disorder

It's important to distinguish both major depression and PDD from another disorder known as **bipolar mood disorder** (formerly called 'manic-depression'). This is a rarer condition where individuals experience a cycle of extremely low and high moods. In other words, they can be depressed at some points (during which time they will exhibit characteristics similar to major depression or PDD), but this is interspersed with periods of high energy and excitement.

When their mood and activity is abnormally high, bipolar individuals may engage in risky or irresponsible behaviour that could be harmful to themselves or to other people.

Key concepts

- Normal
- Abnormal
- Harm
- Distress
- DSM-5
- Major depressive disorder
- Persistent depressive disorder (PDD)
- Bipolar mood disorder

Quick test

1. Why can't psychologists decide what seems normal based only on their own opinion?
2. How long would a person have to show symptoms of major depression in order to be diagnosed according to DSM-5 criteria?

Biological explanations of depression

The role of neurochemistry

Research into the neurochemistry of psychological disorders has suggested that the level of one or more type of neurotransmitter is either too low or too high when someone experiences a disorder, and that this results in their symptoms.

In major depressive disorder, the monoamine neurotransmitter **serotonin** is thought to be at a lower level in depressed patients. It is hard to measure serotonin levels in the living brain, but blood levels are generally lower in depressed individuals. This idea is called the **monoamine hypothesis**, and it is the basis of most drug treatments for depression.

Hormones

Hormones are chemical messengers in the body that regulate many aspects of emotion and behaviour. They can impact on mood in various ways.

- Hormones associated with puberty affect both mood and behaviour in the early teenage years.
- Premenstrual syndrome (PMS) is a mood disturbance associated with the menstrual cycle.
- The thyroid is a gland in the neck that produces hormones. These **thyroid hormones** affect the rate at which the body uses energy. Thyroid hormones can play a role in developing depression.
- Hormones associated with pregnancy can lead to the baby blues – a short-lived depressive state.
- **Postpartum depression** (or 'postnatal depression') is a mood disorder where depression begins after childbirth. Hormonal changes may play a role, though other factors are important too, and the disorder is not fully understood.

The diathesis–stress model

The **diathesis–stress model** states that developing depression depends on a combination of two key things.

- **Diathesis:** a predisposition in someone's biology or thought processes that makes them more vulnerable.
- **Stress:** experiencing stressful or harmful life events.

Often, the diathesis is assumed to be a **genetic predisposition** to developing a disorder. According to diathesis–stress, even identical twins (who have exactly the same genes) may have different mental health outcomes depending on life experiences (see Key study).

Cognition can also be a diathesis (Abramson et al., 1988), that is to say, thought processes can make a person more prone to depression, but developing the disorder (or not) will still depend on life events. Cognitive factors that affect the development of depression are discussed in the final section of this chapter.

📖 Key study: McGuffin et al.'s (1996) twin study of depression

Aim: The researchers wanted to find evidence for the idea that depression has a genetic component.

Method: The researchers studied the UK hospital records of patients with depression, and identified 177 patients who had a twin. They assessed the twins for signs of depression, and also determined whether they were monozygotic (identical) or dizygotic (fraternal) twins.

Findings: In twin studies, concordance means the extent to which both twins have the same trait – in this case, depression. The researchers found a concordance rate of 46% for monozygotic (identical) twins, compared to 20% for the dizygotic twins.

Evaluation: This study provides evidence that genetic factors play a role in depression, but clearly some environmental stressors must play a role too, as there was not a 100% concordance even among the identical twins. The study therefore supports the diathesis–stress model of depression.

Evaluation of biological explanations

Viewing depression in terms of the monoamine hypothesis reduces blame and guilt for the sufferer. However, any neurotransmitter imbalances could be the effect rather than the cause of depression. Viewing depression in biological terms fails to take account of the social processes that contribute.

> 🔍 **Top tip**
>
> You are required to learn at least one study into the biology of depression. McGuffin et al. would be a suitable choice.

The diathesis–stress model combines elements of the different approaches to psychology in a way that has been found to be helpful with various disorders. However, it remains unclear what constitutes a predisposition to develop a psychological disorder. The 'diathesis' could include several things, including genes, mental resilience, personality or a lack of social support. Stress is also a very broad concept. This makes the theory rather vague.

Twin studies have demonstrated a link between genetic relatedness and the chances of developing depression or another disorder. However, it can't be concluded that genes cause these disorders, and no 'depression gene' has been found.

> **Quick test**
>
> 1. Which neurotransmitter is thought to play a role in depression?
> 2. What is meant by the 'diathesis' element of the diathesis–stress theory?

> 🔑 **Key concepts**
>
> - Monoamine hypothesis
> - Thyroid hormones
> - Postpartum depression
> - Diathesis–stress
> - Genetic predisposition

Biological treatments for depression

Drug treatments

The most common treatment for depression is the use of antidepressant drugs. The use of drugs as therapy for a psychological disorder or medical issue is called **chemotherapy** (which simply means chemical therapy).

A huge range of antidepressant medicines have been developed. They all work using similar principles – they are absorbed into the bloodstream and travel into the brain, where they influence the availability of serotonin and/or other monoamine neurotransmitters. They are therefore based on (and also provide evidence for) the monoamine hypothesis.

Drugs can provide relief, but they do not work equally for all patients, and tend to have negative side effects. Drugs could also be viewed as a way of reducing the symptoms of a disorder, rather than tackling the cause.

Some of the main drug therapies for depression are as follows.

Treatment and mechanism	Characteristics
SSRIs (selective serotonin reuptake inhibitors) bind to receptors in brain cells that release serotonin, reducing those cells' ability to re-uptake serotonin. This causes more of this neurotransmitter to be available in the brain.	• Frequently prescribed • Highly effective • Affects serotonin levels • Relatively mild side effects that can include nausea, agitation, sleep quality and sexual dysfunction • Linked to suicidal thoughts in rare cases
SNRIs (serotonin-norepinephrine reuptake inhibitors) SNRIs work in the same way as SSRIs, but they affect another mood-related neurotransmitter – norepinephrine – as well as serotonin.	• Frequently prescribed • Highly effective • Affects levels of serotonin AND norepinephrine • Side effects similar to SSRIs • Similar efficacy to SSRIs
Tricyclics block the action of a protein that transports serotonin back to the neuron that has released it. This increases the level of serotonin available at synapses.	• Outdated – only now prescribed when SSRIs/SNRIs don't work • Similar efficacy to SSRIs but worse side effects • Side effects include blurry vision, constipation, memory impairments and increased body temperature
MAOIs (monoamine oxidase inhibitors) work by inhibiting the hormone monoamine oxidase. Monoamine oxidase clears excess serotonin, norepinephrine and dopamine from the brain. Inhibiting it therefore increases the availability of these neurotransmitters.	• More often used for anxiety or bipolar disorder than major depressive disorder • Side effects can include high blood pressure • MAOIs interact badly with other drugs • **RIMAs** (reversible inhibitors of monoamine oxidase A) are a newer generation of MAOIs that have improved efficacy and low side effects, but more research is needed

Electro-convulsive therapy

Electro-convulsive therapy (ECT) is a controversial treatment for depression, which has also been used for some other disorders.

- ECT involves passing an electric current through the patient's brain.
- This triggers a form of seizure.
- It is done under local anaesthetic.
- Sometimes it is done against a patient's will.
- ECT results in disorientation to the patient.
- ECT modifies blood flow in the frontal lobe of the brain.

ECT is an invasive therapy that can cause distress and memory loss. For this reason, it is not used routinely. However, it is considered an option for the most severely depressed patients, especially those who are considered a suicide risk, and who have not responded to antidepressant drugs of the types discussed above.

Read and Arnold (2017) conducted a systematic review of over 90 studies of ECT. They found that although there is some evidence of the therapy's effectiveness during the course of treatment, it was no more effective than a placebo treatment beyond that point. They concluded that ECT cannot be scientifically or ethically justified.

Top tip

Drug side effects are specific to the patient – two people may have very different reactions to the same antidepressant. The antidepressant will also work better for some people than others in terms of improving the symptoms of depression.

Key concepts

- Chemotherapy
- SSRIs (selective serotonin reuptake inhibitors)
- SNRIs (serotonin-norepinephrine reuptake inhibitors)
- Tricyclics
- MAOIs (monoamine oxidase inhibitors)
- RIMAs (reversible inhibitors of monoamine oxidase A)
- Electro-convulsive therapy (ECT)

Quick test

1. Which two types of drug are most commonly used for major depression today?
2. What effect does ECT have on blood flow in the brain?

Cognitive explanations of depression

Beck's cognitive triad

The cognitive approach to depression states that it can be explained and therefore treated on the basis of thoughts and beliefs. Aaron Beck (1976) stated that depressed people have a negative **cognitive triad** – three key negative beliefs about:

- themselves
- the world
- the future.

These need to be tackled in order to change a person's mood or behaviour.

Negative self-schemas

Beck believed that depressed people have biased thoughts, particularly about themselves, such as:

- **personalisation**: unduly relating all events to oneself
- **overgeneralisation**: thinking that an event will apply to all situations
- **selective abstraction**: focusing on only one aspect of an event.

Depressed people have learned a pattern of negative rather than positive habits of thought, possibly early in life. These are based on **negative self-schemas**. As schemas are resilient cognitive structures, it's very difficult to persuade a depressed individual that their self-schemas are inaccurate.

Faulty information processing

Albert Ellis also believed that depression should be treated by tackling problematic cognitions through therapy. His **ABC model** argued that an activating event (A) is followed by a belief about that event (B), and then emotional consequences (C). If beliefs are irrational, this can have harmful emotional consequences.

Alloy et al. (1999) investigated the thinking style of students without depression, and then followed them up over five years. They found that 17% of those who had shown a negative thinking style later developed depression, compared to 1% of the positive thinking group. This is evidence that cognitive processes can be a form of diathesis (see previous section), making people more vulnerable.

CBT

Ellis and Beck developed **cognitive-behavioural therapy** (CBT), a psychotherapy that aims to modify thought processes. CBT draws on both the behaviourist and the cognitive approach to psychology:

- cognitive aspects focus on a rational discussion of the client's beliefs
- behaviourist techniques attempt to change habits and make new associations.

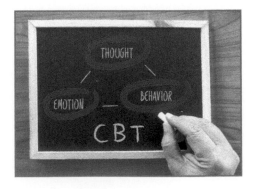

The CBT therapist discusses a client's beliefs and tries to get them to see things more rationally. This process is called **cognitive restructuring**. CBT therapists make use of numerical rating scales to get a quick assessment of how their client is feeling about specific situations.

📖 Key study: The treatment of adolescents with depression ('TADS') study by the National Institute of Mental Health (March et al., 2007)

Aim: The aim of the study was to test the effectiveness of major treatments for depression for teenagers and establish whether the benefits of antidepressants outweighed the risks in teens.

Method: The study was a drug trial, comparing an antidepressant drug with CBT. There were also groups who had both (antidepressant and CBT) and a control group who took a placebo pill. The drug used was an SSRI. Participants were 439 school pupils aged 12–17.

Findings:

- At 12 weeks, antidepressants led to a bigger improvement than CBT (61% vs. 44% were 'much improved').
- At 18 weeks, CBT had caught up (65% for antidepressants vs. 62% for CBT).
- Both therapies were better than the placebo.
- The longer the treatment went on, the better the CBT group did.
- The best outcomes came from a combination of both antidepressants and CBT.
- However, the drugs led to negative side effects including new suicidal thoughts (found in no other group).

Evaluation: This study was longitudinal and conducted on a large scale. It made a carefully controlled comparison of three main interventions. A strength is that it included students from many schools. It is limited in that it did not study other types of therapy/counselling.

Evaluation

A strength of cognitive theories is that they examine the root of the problem rather than focusing on symptoms. However, it's possible that low mood is the cause of some negative thought processes and beliefs, rather than the reverse.

CBT is a quick and effective therapy. Its strengths have led to it becoming the main choice of psychotherapy on the NHS, as well as internationally. CBT has been found to work best in combination with chemotherapy. When used alone it has no biological side effects, although it is possible that some of the exercises undertaken could cause psychological side effects such as frustration or embarrassment.

> 🔍 **Top tip**
>
> You are required to learn at least one study into cognitive causes or treatment of depression. The TADS study would be a suitable choice.

> 🔑 **Key concepts**
>
> - (Negative) cognitive triad
> - Negative self-schemas
> - Faulty information processing
> - Personalisation
> - Overgeneralisation
> - Selective abstraction
> - ABC model
> - Cognitive-behavioural therapy
> - Cognitive restructuring

Quick test

1. What three negative beliefs are included in Beck's 'negative cognitive triad'?
2. Which therapy works best in the long term, according to TADS?

Memory

3 Memory

The nature of memory

Memory stores

Memory is not a single process in the mind. Instead, there are multiple different memory stores, each responsible for remembering different types of information. Three important stores to be aware of are:

! **Syllabus note**

This topic is in the Individual Behaviour unit. Higher Psychology students must study Depression <u>or</u> Memory <u>or</u> Stress.

- **Sensory memory:** this is a very brief form of memory that retains things that we see and hear long enough for us to focus our attention on them. A good example of using sensory memory is when a person speaks to you and you are not paying attention. If you switch your attention and focus on what they have just said, you will probably find that you can still remember it.

- **Working memory (WM):** this store (also called short-term memory (STM) or primary memory) can hold a short list of items, and can also use and manipulate information. WM is very limited in its duration, but information can be retained as long as we are using it in some way. WM can only hold a few words or numbers at a time. An example of using working memory would be responding to a request for directions – this would involve maintaining a person's question in mind while mentally picturing a route, and formulating a suitable response; (see page 54 'The working memory model' for more about this system).

- **Long-term memory (LTM):** this is the mind's system for permanently storing factual information, and retains word meanings more effectively than the sounds of words (Baddeley, 1966). However, it can also retain life events (episodic memory) and skills (procedural memory). LTM stores information in interconnected sets of knowledge called schemas.

As can be seen, each of the three basic memory stores described above actually comprises several sub-stores. These sub-stores are based in different brain areas.

Memory processes

Regardless of which memory store (or sub-store) is being studied, a logical set of processes must take place:

- **Encoding** involves taking information from the senses or from another memory store and placing it into a memory code. Different memory stores use different types of code/coding (see below).

- **Storage** involves retaining information to be used at a later point. In the case of the shorter-term stores, this involves attention and/or rehearsal.

- **Retrieval** is where information is brought back from the memory store when needed.

🔍 **Top tip**

Some psychologists use the terms working memory and short-term memory interchangeably, while others state that STM relates to storage alone and WM relates to both storage and processing. It is therefore fine to talk about working memory if asked to explain short-term memory in the exam but it's always best to briefly define terms that you use.

Types of coding

One key feature of each memory store is the type of memory 'code' or information that it processes. A traditional view of the types of coding used by different stores is outlined below.

○ **Top tip**

Note that several key elements in memory come in threes – three processes, three stores, three types of LTM. Can you find any more?

- There are different types of coding in sensory memory, one for each sense.
- Working (or 'short-term') memory uses **acoustic** (sound-based) coding.
- Long-term memory uses **semantic** (meaning-based) coding.

However, it is now clear that working memory and LTM can each use more than one type of coding, depending on the situation. Working memory has a visual sub-system (Baddeley and Hitch, 1974), and long-term memory can store events and procedures, in addition to facts. We also know that long-term memory can process and store some visual information.

Name of store	Capacity	Duration	Main type of coding	Role of visual and verbal encoding
Sensory memory	Large – all information reaching the senses at any given time	Very brief – two seconds or less	Multiple, one for each sense	Visual information fades more rapidly than verbal
Working memory (previously called short-term store/short-term memory)	Limited to four discrete items or a list lasting around two seconds	Information can be retained while still in use but otherwise fades after 30 seconds or less	Acoustic, but depends on the information being processed	Processes visual and verbal information simultaneously in many everyday tasks
Long-term memory (LTM)	Unlimited	Effectively unlimited, but subject to forgetting	Semantic (meaningful information), but other modalities can also be retained	Dual coding makes it easier to memorise new information

Key concepts

- Sensory memory
- Working memory (WM)
- Long-term memory (LTM)
- Encoding
- Storage
- Retrieval
- Acoustic encoding
- Semantic encoding
- Visual encoding

Quick test

1. Name two of the sub-stores of LTM.
2. What are the three stages of the memory process?

The multi-store model

The **multi-store model** or MSM is a useful but simplistic model devised by Atkinson and Shiffrin (1968). It features the main stores described above – sensory memory, working memory (originally called the 'short-term store' in the model), and long-term memory.

The model does recognise that these stores had different sub-stores for different types of information, such as the different types of sensory memory. However, it doesn't present these in any detail.

A key aspect of the model and one of its most useful features is that it describes how the stores connect together. The model makes two main claims about this:

- Information is transferred from sensory memory into WM by a process of paying **attention** to it.
- Information is transferred from working memory into LTM by a process of maintenance **rehearsal** of the information, thereby keeping it in mind for longer.

This leads to a prediction that information will only be retained over the long term if it has been rehearsed or used in working memory for a period of time. According to this view, the key factor that leads to information being encoded to LTM (and therefore the factor affecting all new learning) is the amount of processing that takes place.

The process of maintenance rehearsal also plays a role in keeping information in working memory for longer. It could involve saying words over again and again, for example. You have experienced this if you have ever repeated words and phrases to yourself when trying to learn lines or quotes from a play, or when trying to remember a shopping list.

When information is retrieved from LTM it travels back to WM in order to be used.

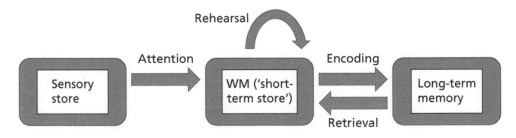

Research evidence and evaluation – MSM

The idea of a separate working memory and LTM is supported by the **serial position effect** (composed of the primacy and recency effects). Glanzer and Cunitz (1966) suggested that the primacy effect is due to rehearsal of the first few items, while recency is due to recall of the later items that are still held in working memory (see Key study).

Neurological evidence from brain scans and patients with brain damage also supports the idea of a separate WM and LTM, because it appears that people can have damage to one of these stores and not the other.

Craik and Tulving (1975) showed that words were better recalled if questions were asked about their meaning, rather than about their appearance (such as 'is it in capital letters?'), showing that meaningless 'rote' rehearsal is not the best way of encoding information to LTM.

Aim: This experiment aimed to show that memory uses more than one process when remembering a list, providing evidence for the idea that short-term/working memory and LTM are separate.

Methodology: Participants were given lists of random words to remember. The shortest lists were 10 items long, and the longest lists were 40 items long.

Findings: The study found that words at the start of the list were better remembered than those in the middle. This is known as the primacy effect. Words at the end were better remembered, too – this is called the recency effect. In combination these effects are known as the serial position effect.

Evaluation: This study played a role in the development of the MSM. However, its use of random lists of words means that it lacks mundane realism, and the researchers didn't test other types of items or study long-term retention of the words.

Evaluation – MSM

The MSM is a useful overview of the main memory stores and how they link together. The idea that attention is necessary for items to be encoded to memory is generally accepted.

On the negative side, the model is too simplistic, as both WM and LTM are actually composed of several components.

The model was one of the first to present a working memory that engaged in the processing of information. However, it was still seen mainly as a **passive** store, and this has been superseded by Baddeley's working memory model (see next section).

The idea of items entering LTM due to rehearsal is flawed. It is possible to rehearse items and still forget them.

> 🔍 **Top tip**
>
> You are required to learn at least one study relevant to the MSM. Murdock (1962) would be a suitable choice.

Quick test

1. Name the research study that cast doubt on the MSM by showing that meaningful processing was more important than rehearsal.

🔑 Key concepts

- Multi-store model
- Attention
- Rehearsal
- Passive
- Serial position effect

The working memory model

In the early 1970s, researchers Alan Baddeley and Graham Hitch tried to replace the MSM, which they saw as limited and inaccurate. Their model, the working memory model (or WMM) shows working memory as a system for carrying out tasks, not merely a memory 'store'.

Overview of the model

A component called the **central executive** controls the other parts of the model, which are known as **slave systems**.

The central executive is responsible for decision making and carrying out complex processes. It is the part of our mind that allocates attention to tasks. As attention is limited, the central executive selects what to focus on.

The most recent version of the model (Baddeley, 2000) shows three slave systems:

- the **phonological loop** – verbal working memory
- the **visuo-spatial sketchpad** – visual working memory
- the **episodic buffer**, responsible for binding sensory information into meaningful events – it is a passive store, and links working memory with LTM.

In each system, the processing time to do tasks is based on real time. For example, following a pattern in your head (using your visuo-spatial sketchpad) takes as long as it would take to trace your finger around it.

Name of WM system	Function	Main type of coding	Capacity
Phonological loop	Process and briefly store language	Verbal/acoustic	Two seconds pronunciation time as a rehearsal loop
Visuo-spatial sketchpad	Process and briefly store images and spatial information	Visual	A single complex pattern
Episodic buffer	Combine information from other parts of WM and from LTM into a coherent event	Multiple	Limited – one or two episodes
Central executive	Executive control of other systems; novel/creative processes	Based on attention and can use multiple forms of code where required	Essentially no storage capacity – processing only

Research into WMM

Baddeley et al. (1973) asked participants to trace a 'hollow letter F' with a pointer. This was done at the same time as a verbal task without any deficit to either task. However, when participants tried to do two visual tasks at the same time, performance dropped significantly. Therefore, multi-tasking is only possible if it uses more than one slave system.

Hitch and Baddeley (1976) found that the central executive can perform verbal decision-making when the phonological loop is occupied.

Baddeley et al. (1975) found that the number of words that could be held in working memory depended on the length of the word (see Key study). This fits with the principle that cognitive processing is done in real time.

📖 Key study: Baddeley, Thomson and Buchanan (1975) – the word length effect

Aim: *Baddeley et al. were looking for evidence that processing time in working memory is equivalent to real-world task time, and also wanted to reconsider the storage capacity of working memory.*

Method: *The study tested short-term recall of lists of words by giving people groups of five words that were either short (e.g. 'book') or long (e.g. 'university'). Participants were asked to recall the first three letters.*

Findings: *The researchers found that the number of words that could be held in working memory depended on the length of the word – the longer the words, they fewer could be retained.*

Evaluation: *The research helped to distinguish between the two main models of memory. As a lab experiment it was well controlled, though rather artificial. The findings have been supported by other studies, including comparisons of bilingual English and Welsh speakers.*

Evaluation of WMM

The model has been able to integrate a large number of research findings such as the 'word length effect', and represents an advance on unitary, passive models of short-term memory.

The model has been usefully applied in education and language development, for example by Gathercole and Baddeley (1990).

🔍 Top tip

You are required to learn at least one study relevant to the working memory model. Baddeley et al. (1975) would be a suitable choice. It could potentially be used as evidence *against* MSM, if asked to evaluate that model.

🔑 Key concepts

- Central executive
- Slave system
- Phonological loop
- Visuo-spatial sketchpad
- Episodic buffer

Quick test

1. What is the central component of the WMM called?
2. Which part of WM deals with verbal information?

Forgetting

Trace decay

One explanation of forgetting is that a stored memory trace simply fades away over time. This process is known as **trace decay**.

Trace decay theory has been applied to all of the three main memory stores, but in different ways:

- Sensory memory has a strictly limited duration. Words that you hear will decay in two seconds or less, and images even more rapidly.

- Working memory is limited to a maximum of 30 seconds (usually less), after which information is lost unless it is rehearsed (Peterson and Peterson, 1959).

- Decay in LTM could involve information being slowly lost over days, weeks or years.

> Atkinson and Shiffrin (1968) thought that LTM forgetting was partly due to decay. However, Bjork (1994) argued that items are not forgotten but simply lose retrieval strength, meaning that they become harder to retrieve.

Applications

Decay theory can inform how you approach your studies:

- As information will decay rapidly from sensory memory or working memory, it is necessary to encode new items to LTM.

- Information in LTM may also decay unless it is revised periodically, preferably via active retrieval that is spaced out over time.

- Rather than having decayed, some items studied might not have been properly learned in the first place, perhaps because they were presented too quickly or never fully understood.

- Koriat et al. (2004) showed that learners underestimate how quickly they will forget information.

> 🔍 **Top tip**
>
> Ensure that you can link decay to all three memory stores. It is best if you can be specific about the duration involved, and why information might be lost from each one.

Evaluation

Waugh and Norman (1965) investigated the role of decay in working memory by varying the speed at which a list of items were read. This was found to make only a slight difference, and they concluded that short-term forgetting is mainly due to information being displaced from working memory by new information, rather than due to decay.

It is widely assumed that memories decay over time in LTM, but the alternative view that they simply become less accessible is also popular.

Many research studies into decay have used arbitrary and meaningless information, and don't fully allow for the different parts of working memory that are shown in Baddeley's working memory model.

Interference

When things are unique or at least very distinctive, it's much easier to remember them. However, similar material and ideas are easily mixed up in LTM. This type of forgetting is called **interference**.

There are two types of interference.

- **Retroactive interference** is where new information interferes with old, such as finding it hard to remember your old address, or what rooms your classes were in a couple of years ago.

- **Proactive interference** is when old information interferes with new information, such as looking for something where it used to be kept, or using an older name for someone who has changed their name.

Top tip

Prepare simple real-world examples of the different types of forgetting. You can use these in exam answers.

Evidence and evaluation

A study by Baddeley and Hitch (1977) found better recall of games among rugby players who had experienced injuries. This supports interference theory, as they had played in fewer games, leading to less interference with their memories.

Interference fits well with the information processing model in cognitive psychology, but doesn't fit so well with the view of LTM as an unlimited passive store.

Contrary to the theory, experts can learn a lot about one topic without suffering from interference. This could be because they have better-developed schemas, making them less prone to mixing up concepts that seem similar to novices.

Top tip

In the exam, you can pick up analysis marks by comparing different theories of forgetting to each other, and giving real-world examples.

Cue-dependent forgetting

Forgetting can occur if information is stored in LTM but a person is unable to retrieve it. This type of forgetting is more likely to happen if there are no cues to help retrieval. For this reason, it is known as cue-dependent forgetting.

There are three types of cues that can affect memory and forgetting.

- **State cues:** being in the same physical state as when information was learned.

- **Context cues:** being in the same place where information was learned.

- **Verbal cues**, such as a letter or word that triggers a memory.

Evidence

Consuming a drug such as alcohol or marijuana changes a person's physical state, and people will be more prone to forgetting if they are in a different state compared to when information was learned. Duka et al. (2001) found that being in the same state improved performance on a word recall task, but that automatic aspects of memory were unaffected.

Godden and Baddeley (1975) showed the role of context cues in an experiment where people learned word lists either on land or underwater. Retrieval was significantly better in the same context as where lists had been learned.

The tip-of-the-tongue phenomenon demonstrates the importance of verbal cues. People typically get a sense that they can almost recall the word, while a cue such as the first letter of the word is often enough to prompt recall.

Evaluation

Cue-dependent forgetting applies only to LTM, because the other memory stores only hold information that we are currently aware of.

The theory has practical consequences – it suggests that for students, it would be easier to retrieve information that has been learned in multiple, varied contexts.

> **🔍 Top tip**
>
> Use the concept of cue-dependent forgetting to help you revise.

Forgetting due to brain damage

Biological psychologists think that that all memories are based in the brain. Therefore, if a person experiences **brain damage**, forgetting can occur.

Certain brain areas are particularly important for memory processes.

- The hippocampus is essential for encoding new memories to LTM.
- The frontal lobes of the neocortex play a key role in attention and executive processes in working memory.
- Visual areas of the neocortex are essential for the visuo-spatial sketchpad (visual working memory).

Cells in the hippocampus can be affected by stress, but more severe problems occur when it is damaged via injury, illness or a brain operation. Damage to the frontal lobe can harm working memory without impacting on LTM.

Henry Molaison (known as 'H.M.') had his hippocampus removed during surgery. This caused unexpected and permanent damage to his memory (see Key study).

📖 Key study: Scoville and Milner (1957) – the case of H.M.

- *Aim*: Scoville and Milner (1957) aimed to investigate Henry's memory loss, as well as his other cognitive abilities.
- *Method*: The researchers conducted interviews with the patient and his family, and administered a memory test called the 'Wechsler Memory Scale' and an IQ test.
- *Findings*: Henry's personality and IQ were unchanged after the surgery. He could recall his childhood and the events before the operation, but could not encode any new information to LTM. Later research showed that his procedural memory had been unharmed.
- *Evaluation*: The precise nature of Henry's brain damage helped scientists to learn more about the role of the hippocampus in memory. However, the surgery damaged other brain areas, making it hard to be entirely sure which problems were due to the hippocampus. The findings from interviews with family members may have been biased.

Evaluation

Brain injury cases establish the clear role of specific brain areas in memory, and also provide evidence that WM and LTM are largely separate.

However, they don't explain forgetting in everyday situations, which is more often due to a failure to encode information to LTM, interference, decay or a lack of cues.

Top tip

This study can be used as evidence in an answer about forgetting, but could also be described as evidence for the multi-store model.

Quick test

1. Is storing information in working memory a good learning strategy for students?
2. Which type of interference is involved if you accidentally type your old password into a website?
3. Why can it be unclear whether information has decayed in LTM?
4. Name three types of cues.
5. If a person studies late at night in their bedroom while drinking strong coffee and then tries to recall the information the next morning in the exam hall, what memory cue(s) might be different?
6. If a person's hippocampus was damaged in an accident, which of the following is more likely to be affected:
   a) their memories of their childhood
   b) their personality
   c) their ability to learn new facts

Key concepts

- Trace decay
- Interference
- Proactive interference
- Retroactive interference
- State cues
- Context cues
- Verbal cues
- Brain damage

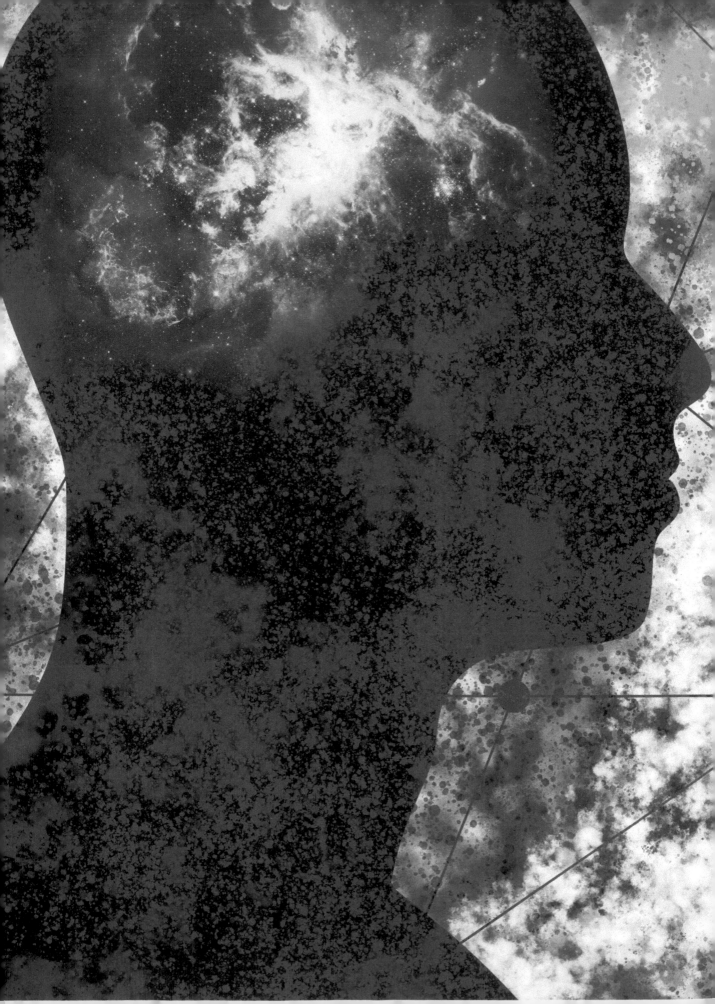

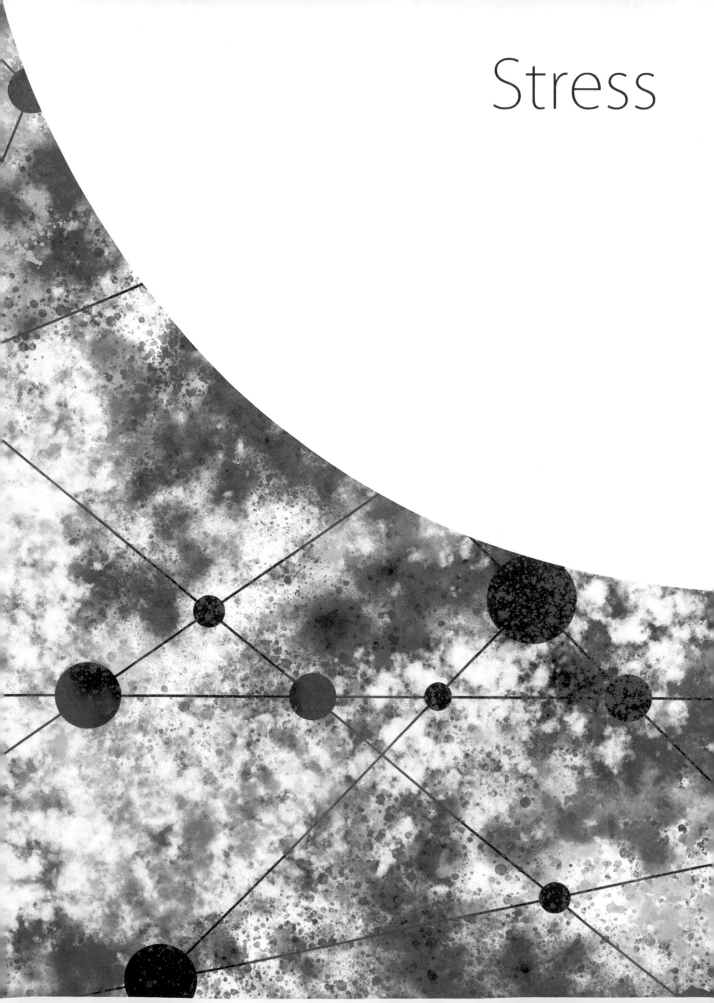

Stress

4 Stress

The physiology of stress

The fight-or-flight response

Sometimes we feel stressed by an immediate threat. This is called **acute stress**. Your body responds to these situations with a **fight-or-flight response**, which involves a release of energy into the bloodstream. You experience sensations such as your heart beating faster, tension in your muscles, fast and shallow breathing, and focused attention on the threat. This evolved response prepares the body for either self-defence ('fight') or running away ('flight').

Explanations of fight-or-flight

We often experience fight-or-flight when it is useless – in situations where we would neither fight nor run away, such as when in a traffic jam or looking at a bank statement. Why does the body produce an unhelpful response to stress?

The explanation is that the fight-or-flight response has evolved over millions of years. It would have helped our ancestors to survive. Many of today's problems have not been around for long enough to make a significant difference to the human gene pool. This helps us to understand why our heart rate rises and we release energy when stressed – even when it is no longer useful.

! Syllabus note

This topic is in the Individual Behaviour unit. Higher Psychology students must study Depression or Memory or Stress.

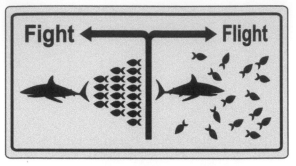

🔍 Top tip

If you are trying to describe fight-or-flight in the exam, think of a situation where you experienced the response.

The general adaptation syndrome

Hans Selye came up with a theory of a **general adaptation syndrome** (GAS). This theory suggests that the fight-or-flight response is only the beginning of a much longer process, through which the body copes with challenges. Selye used the term **stressors** to describe the sources of stress. **Chronic stress** refers to prolonged or repeated stressful situations.

The GAS assumes that the effects of stress are cumulative, and that the amount of stress matters but the nature of the stressors does not.

📖 Key study: Selye's (1936) study of stress in rats

Aim: Selye's experiment subjected rats to different stressors and compared the effects.

Method: The rats were subjected to stressors such as surgical injury, extremes of temperature, and injections of toxic substances such as formaldehyde. These were repeated over many weeks to prevent recovery.

Findings: The animals showed a physiological triad: enlargement of adrenal glands, bleeding from ulcers in the digestive system, and shrinking of lymph tissue (the body areas that produce white blood cells). After 6–48 hours of treatment, these systems returned to normal. After a further 1–3 months, symptoms returned, and the animal became vulnerable to disease. The response to all of the stressors was the same.

Stages of the syndrome

1. **Alarm** reaction: the body experiences fight or flight. The body's adrenal glands enlarge, and stomach ulcers may develop. The lymph (white blood cell) system shrinks, harming the immune response. This stage can last for several hours.
2. **Resistance:** the body adapts to the presence of the stressor and alarm stage symptoms disappear. Energy is obtained by burning fats.
3. **Exhaustion:** if the stress is prolonged, the body may become exhausted. After a month or more, first stage symptoms reappear. There is increased vulnerability to disease and psychological problems.

Evaluation

The GAS is a detailed theory of stress, based on experiments looking at bodily changes. However, a lot of the supporting research has been done on animals, making it hard to generalise to humans. Also, the use of very extreme physical stressors in Selye's 1936 study makes it hard to generalise the findings to the stressors we encounter during everyday life.

More recently, the idea that all stressors produce the same physiological response has been challenged. It may be that this is the case only when the stressors are at an unusually high level (Goldstein and Kopin, 2007).

Key concepts

- Acute stress
- Chronic stress
- Fight-or-flight response
- General adaptation syndrome
- Alarm, resistance and exhaustion
- Stressor

Quick test

1. The fight-or-flight response involves an animal or person preparing for either self-defence, or what other action?
2. Were there any ethical issues with Selye's research?

Stress and health

The role of hormones

Two hormones in particular are associated with stress.

- **Adrenaline** is released by the adrenal glands during acute stress. This helps the body to prepare for an immediate threat.
- **Cortisol** is released during the resistance stage of GAS. It releases energy in a different way – by using up stored energy from fats and muscles. Cortisol is also released from a different part of the adrenal glands.

The release of adrenaline and cortisol is governed by two different systems in the body, one of which is associated with acute stress, and one of which is associated with chronic stress.

The sympatho-adrenal medullary system

When the body is aroused by a threat, the sympathetic branch of the autonomic nervous system (ANS) becomes active. These nerves stimulate the middle of the adrenal glands (the adrenal medulla) to release adrenaline. Overall, this set of processes is called the **sympatho-adrenal medullary system**. When a threat has passed, the parasympathetic branch of the ANS becomes active, and triggers the body to relax — to 'rest and digest'.

The hypothalamic–pituitary–adrenal system

There is also a slower response to stress. This involves the hypothalamus in the brain, which instructs the pituitary gland to release a messenger hormone called ACTH, which in turn stimulates the release of cortisol from the outer part of the adrenal glands (the adrenal cortex – from which the term 'cortisol' derives). This set of processes is called the **hypothalamic–pituitary–adrenal system**. It is a slower response than the sympatho-adrenal medullary system because it relies on hormones travelling around the bloodstream rather than on the fast connections of the nervous system.

Health effects

Short-term health effects of stress include:

- being more susceptible to infections such as the common cold
- becoming moody and irritable
- having difficulty concentrating
- finding it hard to sleep.

Long-term health effects of stress include:

- raised blood pressure (hypertension)
- increased risk of diseases of adaptation such as coronary heart disease (CHD) and coronary artery disease
- slower wound healing
- skin conditions can worsen

> 🔍 **Top tip**
>
> The sympatho-adrenal medullary system and the hypothalamic–pituitary–adrenal system are often labelled 'SAM' and 'HPA'.

> 🔍 **Top tip**
>
> The hypothalamus also triggers the release of the sleep hormone melatonin, but a different gland is involved — the pineal gland.

> **Make the link**
>
> Cortisol is also called hydrocortisone, and is used medically as a steroid cream. Its ability to reduce the immune response makes it helpful in tackling inflammation or allergic reactions.

- unhealthy behaviours such as overeating, smoking or drinking become more likely
- greater susceptibility to anxiety and depression
- increased risk of eating disorders.

Physical health effects are largely side effects of the physical changes that occur during the stress response. Both adrenaline and cortisol boost glucose levels in the bloodstream. When this extra energy is not used, it can cause damage to arteries and to the heart.

Immunosuppression

High levels of cortisol in the bloodstream can harm the **immune system**. A key part of the immune system is the lymph (or lymphatic) system, which produces white blood cells (also called 'leucocytes'). If stress is prolonged over several days or more, the production of key virus-fighting white blood cells reduces. This makes the body more vulnerable to infection. This is termed **immunosuppression**.

Kiecolt-Glaser et al. (1984) investigated immunosuppression among students around their exam time. In a study of 75 first-year medical students, the researchers collected blood samples a month before the exams and again at exam time. They also give out a stress questionnaire.

It was found that students had lower levels of 'killer T' virus-fighting white blood cells during the exams, making them more vulnerable to illness. The questionnaire confirmed that this was a time of higher stress, particularly for those without a strong social support network.

A possible factor for the harm caused by stress is that unlike other species, modern humans do not engage in physical activity when faced with threats, a situation that differs from our evolutionary past. Exercise can prevent some of the negative health effects of stress by reducing the suppression of leucocytes.

Key concepts

- Adrenaline
- Cortisol
- Sympatho-adrenal medullary system
- Hypothalamic–pituitary–adrenal system
- Immune system
- Immunosuppression

Quick test

1. Which has the more serious effect on health – acute or chronic stress?
2. Name two psychological disorders where stress can play a role.
3. What term means that the function of the immune system is reduced?

Sources of stress

Types of stressor

Stressors can be categorised into three main types:

- **social**: stress from interactions with other people
- **occupational**: stress from our work or studies
- **environmental**: stress from our surroundings, such as noise.

It is useful to know these terms, but they are not well-defined categories and they often overlap. For example, arguing with a fellow student about a research project is both an occupational and a social stressor.

Research into sources of stress

Environmental

Every day, people are exposed to a lot of noise, much of it outwith our control. This can have various negative effects.

- It can impact on healthy development.
- Children in noisier homes show more frustration at school tasks.
- Children from noisier homes have higher overnight levels of cortisol.
- If noise is unpredictable, this increases its stressful effects.

Another major environmental stressor is overcrowding. Anyone who has had to take a long journey on a crowded bus or train knows how tense this can make you feel. Calhoun (1962) conducted a longitudinal observational study into the effects of overcrowding on rats.

- Rats were allowed to breed in a 10 foot by 14 foot enclosure.
- In time, the enclosure became overcrowded with 80 rats in a space meant for 48.
- Many rats became depressed and unresponsive.
- Females failed to build nests or look after their offspring.
- Some rats cannibalised or sexually assaulted others, sometimes attacking them in gangs.
- The mortality rate was very high.

While it is hard to generalise from rats to humans, the findings suggest that the stress of overcrowded conditions can dramatically impact on mental health and lead to antisocial behaviour.

Occupational

Research by Marmot et al. (1997) in the British Civil Service found that the managers at the top of the workplace hierarchy had the lowest level of illness, and the illness level increased with each rank down the hierarchy. Lower ranked workers had less **control** over their work.

Sapolsky (1995) found similar health changes in baboon hierarchies – lower-ranked individuals in the group were more stressed and less healthy. This suggests that less power and control leads to more stress, and consequent ill-health.

Workload also plays a role.

- Traditional views such as the GAS model (see previous sections) would suggest that more work will lead to more stress, because stress was seen as cumulative.
- Other factors besides workload that can raise stress include having a lot of responsibility, doing monotonous work and working in social isolation.
- Workers who experience these occupational stressors tend to take more time off sick.

🔍 **Top tip**

Control is a key concept in workplace stress. Lack of control has been linked to health problems in multiple studies.

Social

Humans are highly social animals; we suffer stress from being isolated, yet our stressors can also come from social interactions.

Rahe et al. (1970) studied a range of major social stressors using a questionnaire called the **social readjustment rating scale (SRRS)**. This included many life events that involved some kind of adjustment to a person's routine, such as:

- divorce
- marriage
- retirement
- pregnancy
- being fired
- death of a friend
- change of school
- holiday
- jail term
- taking out a loan

Rahe and colleagues found a positive correlation between the number of stressors a person had experienced and their level of ill-health. The correlation was weak, perhaps because there are so many other factors that affect health, but it was significant.

This work helped psychologists to assess the impact of life events more accurately. However, the SRRS questionnaire does not account for the differences in severity of the items on the list, and makes no distinction between positive and negative life events or how people feel about the stressors.

Later researchers have found that minor **daily hassles**, while smaller in scale, can have a larger cumulative effect on health (DeLongis et al., 1982). Daily hassles are minor but frequent stressors such as losing things or being held up in traffic. They are sometimes contrasted with 'uplifts', which are minor positive events, such as receiving a compliment.

Quick test

1. What type of stressor is overcrowding?
2. What was the name of the questionnaire used by Rahe et al. (1970)?
3. Is it better to be at the top or at the bottom of a social or occupational hierarchy, according to the research of Marmot et al? Did Sapolsky's work support this conclusion or not?

🔑 Key concepts

- Social stressors
- Occupational stressors
- Environmental stressors
- Control
- Workload
- SRRS (social readjustment rating scale)
- Daily hassles

Individual differences in stress

Some people are better able to cope with stress than others. Factors that make some people more or less prone to stress – or more resilient and better able to deal with stress when it happens – are called **individual differences**.

Locus of control

As mentioned above, control can play a role in how stressed people feel. Rotter (1966) described two main ways that a person's sense of control can vary.

- An **internal locus of control** means feeling that we are in control of events rather than them happening to us, leading to lower stress.
- An **external locus of control** means that we feel out of control, so things happen to us and there is nothing we can do about it. This leads to more stress.

Folkman et al. (1986) interviewed married couples weekly about their main stressors, and found that those with a high internal locus of control were healthier.

Hardiness

Suzanne Kobasa wanted to know why some workers cope better with stress than others. She believed that some exhibit **hardiness**, meaning greater psychological resilience. This had three characteristics:

- commitment: they were highly committed to work and projects.
- control: hardy people had an internal locus of control.
- challenge: they viewed changes as a challenge rather than a threat.

These features are called the **3 Cs of hardiness**. Kobasa (1979) gave the SRRS questionnaire to executives, and found that those with the same score on the questionnaire experienced different levels of illness, depending on their level of hardiness.

Personality

Personality is thought to be relatively stable across the lifespan. Psychologists try to summarise an individual's personality in terms of a small number of **traits** that can be measured with a personality test.

A trait called **neuroticism** is especially relevant to stress. People with high neuroticism are anxious and self-critical, and tend to get stressed about things that other people might not worry about.

Type A behaviour

Closely linked to personality is the idea that people's behaviour can be classified into different types. Researchers Friedman and Rosenman (1974) focused on two in particular.

- **Type A behaviour:** highly competitive and ambitious with a strong desire for recognition and a tendency to rush things.
- **Type B behaviour:** relaxed, with a lack of ambition or drive and a tendency not to rush or get involved in competitive behaviour.

Type A behaviour was associated with a higher level of stress and a higher level of heart problems such as CHD (see Key study). However, neither Type A nor Type B behaviour was originally seen (by the researchers) as a personality type, as they may be open to change over the lifespan.

Other individual differences

There are sex differences in stress.

- Women release less adrenaline than men do, and it lasts for less time in the bloodstream.
- The hormone oxytocin can lower cortisol, an effect which is boosted by oestrogen and reduced by testosterone.

There are also some age differences.

- Teenagers are more likely to show the symptoms of stress openly compared to older adults.
- People of different ages also experience different stressors.

📖 Key study: Friedman and Rosenman's (1974) study of type A and type B behaviour

Aim: The researchers aimed to find out whether behaviour patterns could be a risk factor in the health effects of stress.

Method: The researchers used interviews and questionnaires to put people into one of two categories. Over 3000 participants were categorised into types, all of whom were males aged 39–59.

Findings: More than eight years later, the researchers studied health outcomes. 70% of those who had developed CHD had previously been classified as type A.

Evaluation: The study was done on men, and the findings can't easily be generalised to women. It didn't take into account possible interactions between men and their life or work circumstances. Nevertheless, it was a large-scale study, the first to show that psychological factors can impact on heart disease.

🔑 Key concepts

- Individual differences
- Locus of control
- Hardiness
- 3 Cs of hardiness
- Personality
- Traits
- Neuroticism
- Type A behaviour
- Type B behaviour

Quick test

1. What type of locus of control is associated with lower stress?
2. What are the three 'Cs' of hardiness?

Coping strategies

There are several ways of tackling stress. Three important options of interest to psychologists include drug therapies, stress inoculation therapy and the role of social support.

Drugs

Drugs that directly tackle the stress response in the body are frequently prescribed by GPs, both for stress and for stress-related problems. They include the following.

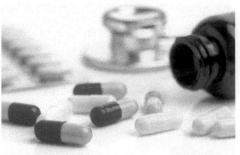

- **Benzodiazepines** such as Valium. These boost a neurotransmitter called GABA, making the person feel more relaxed physically and therefore psychologically.
- **Beta blockers**. These block the 'beta' receptors that respond to adrenaline. This leads to a lower heart rate and reduced blood pressure.

Benzodiazepines tend to cause drowsiness. More severe **side effects** can include confusion, seizures or hallucinations. They are also addictive, so are only recommended for short-term use. Beta blockers have milder side effects and are generally considered safe for longer-term use. They can cause some dizziness and tiredness.

As with other drug therapies for psychological issues, a limitation is that it provides short-term relief without helping to solve underlying problems.

Stress inoculation

Stress inoculation therapy was developed by Donald Meichenbaum and is a specialised form of CBT (see Depression chapter). It teaches the skills needed to help resist stressors using role-playing, visualisation and practice. There are three phases.

- **Conceptualisation phase**: stressors are broken down into smaller units in order to better see how they can be tackled.
- **Skills acquisition phase**: coping skills to deal with specific stressors are taught and practised.
- **Application phase**: newly learned skills are used in real-life stressful situations.

Stress inoculation is effective because people learn to identify the component parts of stress and ways of dealing with them. They learn to tackle stressors in controlled (therapy) situations and are then able to transfer this learning to the real world. It can tackle both chronic and acute stressors, or a complex mixture of both (Meichenbaum, 2007).

A meta-analysis for the United States Army found that stress inoculation reduced performance anxiety and enhanced performance under stressful conditions.

A positive aspect is that it tries to deal with the causes of stress by making people less vulnerable, and teaches real-world strategies. However, the therapy sessions themselves can be time-consuming and expensive; typically, a client would attend sessions once or twice per week for 6–12 weeks.

Social support

People who have better social support tend to have fewer health problems resulting from stress, while those who are isolated suffer more (as was found in the Kiecolt-Glaser et al. study on medical students).

Social support can play two key roles:

- **instrumental** – practical support, such as getting lifts or help with a job application
- **emotional** – support that makes you feel better, like talking and being listened to.

Psychological counselling and therapy tends to offer emotional support rather than instrumental support.

There is a range of evidence suggesting that social support is important in reducing the harmful effects of stress. In a natural experiment, Nuckolls et al. (1972) found that pregnant women under high stress had a much lower rate of pregnancy and birth complications if they had good social support.

Social support can be combined with sport and exercise. Exercise helps people to metabolise the excess glucose that is released into the bloodstream due to stress hormones such as adrenaline. It therefore has biological benefits to the person who is suffering from stress.

A limitation of social support as a coping strategy is that it is reliant on having a good social network. Introverted/isolated people can have great difficulty benefiting from this strategy, as would those who suffer from social anxiety or agoraphobia.

> ## Top tip
> Social support can be either instrumental or emotional.

> ## Key concepts
> - Benzodiazepines
> - Beta blockers
> - Side effects
> - Stress inoculation
> - Conceptualisation phase
> - Skills acquisition phase
> - Application phase
> - Instrumental social support
> - Emotional social support

Quick test

1. Which group of drugs has the more severe side effects, benzodiazepines or beta blockers?
2. What is the first phase of stress inoculation?
3. Give an example of something that might happen in a stress inoculation session.
4. Which type of social support involves tackling a person's problems?

Conformity and obedience

5 Conformity and obedience

The nature of conformity

Conformity can be defined as changing behaviour or beliefs in order to come into line with others in a group. It often results from **peer pressure**, but we can also experience pressure from groups of strangers or from the media.

! Syllabus note

This topic is mandatory for all Higher Psychology students.

Types of conformity

There are three key types of conformity.

- **Compliance** is where a person goes along with a group only while other group members are present, and maintains their own private beliefs.
- **Identification** is where a person temporarily adopts the views or habits of a group, but if they cease to identify as a group member then this conformity will also stop.
- **Internalisation** is where a person permanently adopts the behaviour or beliefs of the group, carries these out away from group situations, and even continues if they stop being a member of the group.

Motivation to conform

Deutsch and Gerrard (1955) proposed two motivating factors behind conformity.

- **Informational influence** – when uncertainty leads to a person adopting the behaviour of others. They conform because they want to be right.
- **Normative influence** – when a person is not in doubt, but is influenced by social norms. They conform because they want to be liked.

O Top tip

Informational and normative influence (also called informational and normative *social* influence) can be credited in exam answers if you are asked to describe *factors* that affect conformity.

Research evidence

Jenness (1932) conducted a study where individuals were asked to guess the number of beans in a bottle. Participants were put in groups of three and asked to give a group estimate after discussion. Most participants later wanted to change their individual guess to a number closer to the group estimate. It appeared that when they feel unsure, people will tend to be influenced by a peer group. This showed informational influence.

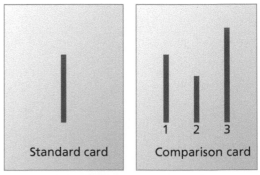

Standard card   Comparison card

Asch used clear images of lines

An experiment by Asch (1951) tested whether conformity would occur even when people could see the correct response clearly (see Key study). Asch's study showed the effects of normative influence.

The study used 'confederates', meaning people who were playing the role of participants, but were actually acting as instructed by the researcher.

Aim: Asch wanted to see whether people would conform to others' incorrect estimates if the task was easy, and the correct answer was obvious. This allowed him to test normative rather than informational influence.

Method: Participants were 50 American men, who were told that this was an experiment into visual perception. Each was placed in a small group, but every other group member was a confederate of the researcher, and had been told how to respond. The group were shown 18 cards, and each time were asked to match one line to a choice of three comparison lines. The confederates all gave the wrong answer on 12 occasions – the 'critical trials'. The true participant was always last or second last to answer.

Findings: Over all critical trials for all participants, incorrect answers were given 32% of the time. A control group made hardly any errors at all. Asch believed that the reason for these findings was that people do not wish to be ridiculed and excluded by a majority. Some participants reported doubting their own perceptions. There were considerable individual differences, with some people conforming nearly every time, while a quarter of participants did not conform at all.

Evaluation: The study was hugely influential, and stimulated other research such as the Mori and Arai experiment (see next section). However, it lacked ecological validity and mundane realism, as neither the setting nor the task were realistic. Some aspects of the findings may be specific to the time and culture tested; Perrin and Spencer (1981) replicated the Asch study using British engineering students, and found a much lower level of conformity.

🔍 Top tip

The 1955 replication/extension of Asch's research found a conformity rate of 36.8 per cent, based on 123 participants. It is fine to use either version as evidence in your exam answers.

Quick test

1. What type of conformity occurs if you feel part of a group, but stops if you leave the group?
2. What type of social influence is motivating your conformity if you join in with a game that you find boring because you don't want to feel left out?
3. Who were the participants in Perrin and Spencer's replication of the Asch study?

🔑 Key concepts

- Conformity
- Peer pressure
- Compliance
- Identification
- Internalisation
- Informational influence
- Normative influence

Factors affecting conformity

The factors that affect conformity can be divided into two types: situational factors and individual differences. Situational factors are aspects of the social situation that affect how much pressure we are put under, while individual differences are things that vary from person to person (such as their age) that affect how susceptible someone is to group pressure.

Situational factors

Group size

The most obvious situational factor is **group size** – a large majority tends to exert more pressure than one or two people do. Asch varied the number of participants in his 'lines' experiment:

- with only one confederate, there was almost no conformity
- with two confederates, the conformity rate was 12.8%
- with three confederates, the rate rose to 33.3%
- the addition of further confederates made only a slight difference to results.

Essentially, Asch found that a majority of three to one was the 'magic number', beyond which further increases had little effect. However, it's possible that true participants became suspicious when large groups all gave the same wrong answer, and in real situations a larger group might have more influence.

> **Top tip**
>
> Note that the overall size of the group is always larger than the number of confederates. For example, with a 3:1 majority, there are three confederates but four people in the group overall, including the minority participant.

Support vs. unanimity

In another variation of Asch's procedure, one confederate acted as an ally to the true participant by disagreeing with the others. The ally was seated fourth, and therefore answered before the true participant.

Total conformity fell to 5.5%, showing that having a group that is **unanimous** exerts a much more powerful influence on our behaviour than one in which there are dissenting voices.

Secrecy of responses

Asch's classic study mainly tested public compliance. In another variation of the lines study, the true participant wrote their answers down privately, while the confederates spoke theirs out loud.

> **Top tip**
>
> In terms of group size, the increase from a two to one majority to a three to one majority has been shown to be critical, and after that, further increases to group size make very little difference.

In this variation, the conformity level fell to 5%. This suggests that compliance is much less likely to occur in real situations where we are able to hide our response.

Task difficulty

Asch's task was easy and obvious, but what would happen if it was made harder? A later replication found that if the lines were made more similar in length, the level of conformity increased. This could be because participants felt less certain, but could also be due in part to their feeling less inhibited about giving wrong answers – if the task is hard, it is less embarrassing to be wrong.

Similarity of group

Abrams et al. (1990) found that if participants feel that they share characteristics with the majority, they are more subject to normative influence in an Asch-type situation. Even just being in the same situation as another person means that we have something in common and may assume that they are similar to ourselves.

This links to the idea of identification – a shared group identity means that we identify with other people, and are more strongly influenced by them.

Top tip

Many of these factors link to words starting with 'S' that could form the basis of a mnemonic: situational: size, support, secrecy, similarity. Task difficulty is the exception!

Individual differences

An important concept in psychology is that people's behaviour is strongly affected by **individual differences** (for example, see the topic of Stress, chapter 4). Some of the main individual differences to consider are age, sex, beliefs, personality and culture.

Age

Conformity levels seem to be high in early-to-middle childhood, and the ability to dissent rises steadily up as we reach early adulthood. The age of the group also affects conformity – as discussed above, similarity is a situational factor in conformity, and we are more likely to conform to people of a similar age to ourselves.

Personality

Certain personality characteristics link to conformity levels.

- In general, people who have higher self-esteem are less likely to conform.

- People who value control are less likely to conform.

Sex

Some researchers have found sex differences in conformity, with women tending to conform more than men. The effect of self-esteem is stronger among males, and makes less of a difference for females (Gergen and Bauer, 1967).

Eagly (1987) has suggested that sex differences can be explained by women trying to promote harmony in a group, while men are more comfortable maintaining independence. However, many studies of gender differences in conformity are culturally biased, and cannot be generalised to all social groups.

Beliefs

Hornsey et al. (2003) found that if someone has a strongly held conviction about an issue, they are less likely to conform. They studied 205 Australian university students who supported same-sex marriage, and showed them faked graphs of other students' views, which apparently showed majority opposition. Privately, those with weak beliefs conformed, while those with stronger beliefs did not. Publicly, the difference was even greater – those with strong beliefs in favour of the topic showed counter-conformity, meaning they became even more strongly in favour of same-sex marriage than before.

Culture

There are numerous ways in which culture can interact with conformity:

- Jenness and Asch both studied young Americans in the 20th century, and findings can't necessarily be generalised beyond that cultural context.

- 1950s America in particular has been described as highly conformist.

- Follow-up studies in other parts of the world have not always replicated Asch's findings.

- Levels of conformity appear to vary from country to country.

- **Collectivist cultures** are those that value family and society over the needs of the individual. They tend to show higher levels of conformity.

- **Individualist cultures** tend to prioritise the likes and wants of the individual over the needs of the group. These cultures tend to show lower levels of conformity.

- The USA is a country with a predominantly individualist culture, while Pakistan is a country with a predominantly collectivist culture.

- Some sub-cultures such as punks are associated with anti-conformity.

> **Top tip**
>
> Ensure that you can explain both situational and individual factors. Cultural factors must also be revised.

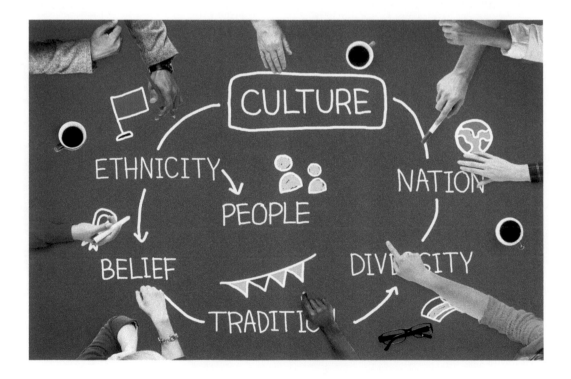

Aim: This study aimed to replicate Asch's experiment without the need for actors. It also included both males and females.

Method: The methodology was very similar to that of the Asch (1951) length of lines study (see previous section). However, the researchers chose not to use confederates. Instead, each participant wore specially designed filter glasses that allow them to look at the same image but see different things. One hundred and four Japanese student participants were used in groups of four, with one member of each group given a different type of filter glasses from the other three. Participants stated their answers out loud, and the minority participant always went third.

Findings: For female participants, results were similar to those of Asch, with conformity to the majority shown at a rate of 36.7%. However, male participants did not conform to a significant extent. Another difference from the Asch findings was that it made very little difference whether the majority were unanimous or not.

Evaluation: The researchers explained the gender difference in terms of the different social expectations of males and females, and they concluded that the reduced conformity in males compared to the Asch study may reflect generational changes since the 1950s. In this study, the participants knew each other; Mori and Arai believe this made the study more relevant to real-world situations.

Analysis

Numerous different factors have been shown to affect conformity. It is important to appreciate that factors can combine – for example, someone could be in a small group and writing their responses in secret. Factors could also work in different directions, with some factors cancelling others out.

In some cases, research evidence conflicts, such as Asch's finding that unanimity was highly impactful compared to Mori and Arai's finding that it didn't make much difference. Of course, both studies could be criticised for using artificial situations.

🔍 **Top tip**

When *analysing* factors, compare the different studies, back up points with evidence, and link ideas to real-world situations.

Quick test

1. At what point in Asch's study did rising majority group size make the biggest difference to conformity?

2. True or false – writing answers in secret made no difference to the conformity level in Asch's study.

3. State two ways in which the research of Mori and Arai (2010) differed from that of Asch.

4. Which group of cultures tends to show higher levels of conformity?

5. How did Mori and Arai (2010) avoid the need for confederates in their study?

🔑 **Key concepts**

- Group size
- Unanimity
- Secrecy
- Similarity
- Individual differences
- Collectivist cultures
- Individualist cultures

Obedience

Obedience involves doing something we are told, or following a rule or instruction. As such, it is another form of social behaviour that results from social pressure. It differs from conformity in several ways.

- Obedience results from pressure from an authority figure, rather than from people similar to ourselves.
- It typically results from a direct order; conformity is usually unspoken.
- It usually involves doing something different from the person giving the order, rather than doing the same as them.
- People are generally happy to admit to obeying, but deny that conformity has affected them.

Obedience can be a useful force in society, as it leads to people following rules and allows organisations to run effectively. However, it can also be harmful. If people obey instructions that are illegal and/or immoral, then obedience becomes problematic.

Legitimate authority

According to social psychologist Stanley Milgram, people are more likely to obey in certain circumstances. These include:

- where there is a **legitimate authority figure** – someone who appears to have the right to tell us what to do
- when the legitimate authority figure takes **responsibility** for the outcome of our actions.

According to Milgram's **agency theory**, these circumstances lead to people making an agentic shift, whereby they pass over control and decision making to the person in charge. This theory therefore contrasts two possible states that we can be in:

- the **autonomous state:** we make our own decisions, and don't obey unreasonable orders
- the **agentic state:** we allow the authority figure to make decisions, and obey all orders, no matter how harmful.

What makes an authority figure legitimate? Many parts of society are structured as hierarchies, meaning that people with lower status are expected to obey those in power, such as a manager in the workplace, or a soldier's commanding officer. These can be seen as formal or legal authorities.

Authority can also derive from:

- social traditions, such as the authority of parents over children – traditional authority can also be based on sex, race or religion
- charisma, where people use their personal charm to convince others to obey them.

Uniform

Even when someone doesn't have a formal authority, they may appear to be an authority because of the way they look. Uniform is one type of clothing that can convey a sense of power and responsibility.

Bickman (1974) put this to the test with an experiment on the streets of New York. In the study, a confederate of the researcher asked passers-by to do menial tasks such as picking up a small coin or a piece of litter. People were more likely to comply when the confederate was dressed in a security guard uniform than in plain clothes.

Milgram's experiment

Milgram conducted a behavioural experiment into obedience which became one of the most famous studies in psychology, as well as being notorious for its ethical flaws. In the experiment, participants were asked to give what they believed were electric shocks to complete strangers, simply to measure the extent to which they would obey an authority figure (see Key study).

Milgram's experiment was motivated by the real-world obedience of Nazis during the Second World War.

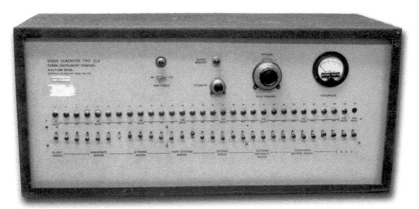

The electric shock apparatus used

📖 Key study: Milgram's (1963) study of obedience

Aim: Milgram wanted to know if there was something uniquely obedient about the Nazi soldiers and concentration camp guards who had carried out the Holocaust. He aimed to discover whether ordinary American citizens would obey an authority figure when asked to inflict pain.

Method: Milgram recruited 40 volunteers. Each was introduced to a fellow participant, 'Mr Wallace', who was actually a confederate. They were told that one of them would be the 'teacher' and one the 'learner' in a memory experiment. The teacher would have to give an electric shock to the learner each time they got an answer wrong. The pair drew lots – but this was fixed so that Mr Wallace was always the learner, and the true participant the teacher. The experimental apparatus had a series of switches, the first of which was labelled 15 volts, and the last 450 volts. Participants were asked to increase the shock level with each wrong answer. The confederate deliberately got many answers wrong, and the participant was under pressure to keep giving stronger shocks.

Findings: All participants continued to give shocks up to a certain point. If the true participant hesitated, the researcher prompted them to continue. The confederate yelled in apparent distress as the faked shocks continued, eventually shouting that he refused to take any further part in the experiment. Despite this, 26 participants (65%) continued up to the maximum shock level of 450 volts. Many showed signs of stress, but none stopped before 300 volts.

Evaluation: This ground-breaking and highly influential study was well controlled. It can be criticised on ethical grounds, as participants were both stressed and deceived. In his defence, Milgram stated that 84% of participants later said that they were glad to have been in the experiment. There may also be some doubt as to whether Milgram's participants really believed in the electric shocks, and if the results *would be found in the real world. However, Hofling et al. (1966) conducted a field experiment in a hospital, in which nurses received a phone call from an unknown doctor calling himself 'Dr Smith'. The doctor told the nurse to prepare and administer a drug with double the indicated maximum dosage. Despite having the opportunity to refuse, 21 out of 22 nurses were going to administer it until stopped by the experimenter. This suggests that the Milgram study's findings are applicable to real situations.*

In a similar way to the Asch experiment (see previous section), the Milgram experiment was changed in various ways in order to test the situational factors that affect obedience. In each case, the obedience level was defined as the percentage of participants who delivered the maximum electric shock, and could be compared with the baseline of 65% from the original study (Milgram, 1974).

Legitimate authority

The original study was carried out in a prestigious Yale University setting. Milgram (1974) replicated it in a downtown office setting, with the experimenter wearing casual clothes. Obedience rate dropped a little to 47.5%, suggesting that the clothing and status of the experimenter was relevant but was not the main cause of obedience.

Proximity

The **proximity** variation repeated the original study but with the teacher sitting in the same room as Mr Wallace. Obedience fell, but only to 40%. Even when the teacher had to hold Mr Wallace's arms down to receive the 'shocks' (the 'touch proximity' condition), there were still 30% who obeyed to the maximum level.

A photograph from the study

Presence of authority

In a 'remote authority' variation, the experimenter gave initial instructions and then left the room, delivering further instructions and answering participant queries by phone. The obedience rate fell to 20.5%.

Peers

Milgram added two confederate teachers who dissented at specific points (150 volts and 210 volts). The obedience rate fell to 10%. In another variation, a confederate teacher pressed the electric shock switches and the true participant just read the questions. 92.5% continued to the maximum level in this variation (Milgram, 1974).

> ### 🔍 Top tip
> Uniform/clothing can be described as one of the factors that affects obedience.

Effects of society

Socialisation

One of the reasons we enter the agentic state is that society has taught us that respecting and obeying authority figures is the right thing to do. **Socialisation** is the gradual adoption of social norms which results from the cumulative social pressure from family, teachers, peers and other significant people as a child grows up.

Parenting

Parents have a big influence on a child's socialisation, but not all children are raised in the same way.

- **Democratic parenting** encourages children to think for themselves and make rational choices. Rules are not absolute. Children raised this way later show lower levels of obedience, as they are more willing to question authority.

- **Authoritarian parenting** teaches children that obedience to and respect for authority figures is the top priority, and that rules should be obeyed without question. Children raised in this way later show higher levels of obedience.

Quick test

1. True or false – obedience differs from conformity in that it usually follows an order from a person in power rather than unspoken pressure from a peer group.

2. Which of the two states from Milgram's agency theory leads to a higher level of obedience?

3. Which makes more of a difference to obedience levels – the authority figure wearing a uniform, or the authority figure being physically present?

Key concepts

- Obedience
- Legitimate authority figure
- Responsibility
- Agency theory
- Agentic state
- Autonomous state
- Proximity
- Socialisation
- Democratic parenting
- Authoritarian parenting

Prejudice

Intergroup bias and discrimination

In social psychology, the term **ingroup** is used to refer to any group that a person is part of, and **outgroup** means a group that they are not part of. **Prejudice** is an attitude, usually negative, towards another person based on their perceived membership of an outgroup.

! Syllabus note

This topic is in the Social Behaviour unit. Higher Psychology students must study Prejudice <u>or</u> Social Relationships <u>or</u> Aggression.

Intergroup biases

Prejudice can be explained in terms of three types of **intergroup bias**:

- cognitive – people's thoughts and beliefs
- affective – people's feelings
- behavioural – people's actions.

Top tip

There isn't universal agreement about how prejudice should be defined. Some researchers see it purely as an emotional reaction, others include the cognitive aspects such as beliefs, while others see it as a synonym of intergroup bias.

It is possible for a person to display some aspects of intergroup bias but not others. A person could believe that teachers are lazy but not dislike them for it (cognitive but not affective), or they could hate conservatives but never act on their hatred (affective but not behavioural).

Discrimination

Discrimination means treating other people better or worse because of their membership of a group or some personal or physical characteristic. For example, it would be discriminatory to deny a woman a job due to her being pregnant.

Discrimination is strongly associated with certain social groups.

- **Sexism:** discrimination against someone on the basis of their biological sex or perceived gender identity, usually though not always referring to discrimination against women. Some sexist attitudes may appear positive but Glick and Fiske (2001) state that such views link to harmful and violent attitudes towards women.

- **Racism:** prejudice and discrimination against a target on the basis of the race that they are assumed to belong to. Sometimes racism is directed at a specific religious group, such as Muslims (Islamophobia) or Jews (antisemitism).

- **Ageism:** prejudice on the basis of age. This often refers to the elderly, but there is also considerable ageism against younger people. As with sexism, there is a positive/protective form of ageism that is often seen as patronising.

- **Heterosexism:** discriminating against people on the basis of their sexuality, particularly the heterosexual majority showing prejudice against minority sexual orientations. It sometimes includes prejudice against transgender groups or people who identify as queer.

The prevalence and acceptability of prejudice depends on social norms. Abrams and Houston (2006) found that British people surveyed were more likely to admit to prejudiced attitudes against homosexual people, Muslims and women than against disabled people or the elderly.

Direct discrimination

Direct discrimination is doing something knowingly harmful towards a target group. Under the UK Equality Act of 2010, it is against the law to discriminate on the basis of sex, age, race, sexual orientation, religion/beliefs, disability, gender reassignment, marital status and pregnancy. This could include any form of unequal treatment, such as paying them less than their peers.

Indirect discrimination

Indirect discrimination is when policies or rules that ostensibly apply equally to everyone affect some groups in a more harmful way than others. An example of this would be an employer setting a rule that nobody could take any time off work during July. This would apply to everyone, but would be more of a problem for people who have school children to care for.

Indirect discrimination is not always illegal, but there is a legal obligation to show that there is a good reason for it. For example, it is considered an occupational necessity to have a certain level of physical health to work in the police or army.

Key concepts

- Prejudice
- Ingroup
- Outgroup
- Intergroup bias
- Sexism
- Racism
- Ageism
- Heterosexism
- Direct discrimination
- Indirect discrimination

Quick test

1. Give an example of how a religious or ethnic group could be indirectly discriminated against.
2. State one example of a group who commonly experience discrimination.
3. What law makes it illegal to discriminate against people on the basis of their race, age and other 'protected characteristics'?

Explanations of prejudice

Stereotyping

A **stereotype** is an over-simplified, distorted or inaccurate belief about a particular group. As such, a stereotype can be seen as a schema about a social group. People often find it offensive to be judged on the basis of stereotypes.

One explanation for prejudice is that if a person holds negative, inaccurate stereotypes about an outgroup, they are more likely to hate or discriminate against that group.

The process of stereotyping involves generalising from a stereotype to an individual person. This leads to two main problems with stereotyping:

- the stereotype itself may be inaccurate
- even if broadly true, the stereotype might not apply to a specific person.

Effect of stereotypes

- **Stereotype threat** is the awareness of a negative stereotype that leads to poorer performance. Ambady et al. (2001) found that when schoolgirls were reminded of gender differences using a questionnaire, they did more poorly on a maths test compared to a control group. Similar effects have been found with female undergraduates.

- **Stereotype lift** is where a positive stereotype can improve performance. However, this can cause harm by disadvantaging other groups who do not receive the same benefit.

Why do stereotypes form?

People are aware of societal stereotypes even if they do not agree with them. Why do they not reject inaccurate stereotypes? **Cognitive miser theory** states that a stereotype is a mental shortcut, made because people do not make the mental effort to process each person's traits individually. Some evidence for this includes:

- Stereotypes develop early, when our cognitive abilities are still very limited. Play tends to show signs of gender stereotypes from the age of two and ingroup favouritism is strongly apparent from the age of five, even though children don't fully understand group differences.

- Memory research has shown that we remember information better if it fits a stereotype, and tend to forget inconsistent information (Fyock and Stangor, 1994).

However, not everyone agrees with this view. Rutland (1999) states that stereotypes are a meaningful attempt to make sense of the world around us, and that we use them consciously.

Authoritarian personality theory

Some explanations of prejudice focus on the characteristics of the individual, and others focus on the influence of the social situation. The **authoritarian personality theory** of prejudice focuses on individual factors.

The theory was developed around the time of the Second World War to explain the appeal of the Nazis and other **fascist** parties, and it draws on the psychoanalytic approach to psychology. Authoritarian individuals were thought to have repressed anger.

Research evidence

Adorno et al. (1950) developed a questionnaire called the **F-Scale** (fascism scale), to measure fascist sympathies. It consisted of a series of statements taken from previous research participants, such as *'People can be divided into two distinct classes: the weak and the strong'*. Participants had to respond on a scale from 'disagree strongly' to 'agree strongly'.

The scale aimed to measure levels of traits that Adorno et al. believed were associated with this personality type. Five of these traits were:

- conventionalism: traditional social values
- authoritarian submission: submissive attitude to authority
- authoritarian aggression: condemning minorities
- anti-intraception: opposition to imaginative thought
- power and 'toughness': preoccupation with strong versus weak.

People with such traits made perfect followers for fascist politicians. Authoritarians are found to have an extreme belief in the rights of the established authorities, for example being much more likely to tolerate illegal government actions (Altemeyer, 2006).

Evaluation

The theory only explains prejudice in individuals, and struggles to explain society-wide prejudice.

Responses to the F-Scale may have been biased, as 'agree' answers always led to higher F-scores. This makes the findings potentially unreliable.

Only three of the original nine traits reliably correlate together: conventionalism, authoritarian submission and authoritarian aggression.

Altermeyer has suggested replacing the term with **RWA – right-wing authoritarianism**, which he says should be seen as an attitude rather than a personality type.

Quick test

1. What is the connection between schemas and stereotypes.
2. What is the key idea behind cognitive miser theory?
3. What term did Adorno et al. (1950) use to describe a submissive attitude to authority?
4. What does RWA stand for?
5. Where were the statements on the F-scale taken from?

🔑 Key concepts

- Stereotype
- Stereotype threat
- Stereotype lift
- Cognitive miser theory
- Authoritarian personality theory
- Fascism
- F-Scale
- RWA – right-wing authoritarianism

Explanations of prejudice cont'd

Social identity theory

Social identity theory states that people's behaviour is driven by group membership. People make decisions about which groups they are or are not part of, then show prejudice against other groups while trying to put their own group on top.

Tajfel and Turner (1979) stated that people mentally divide the world up into 'them and us', binding up their sense of self with group membership. Then they make biased judgements, and if they perceive that the ingroup is not different or superior enough they will try to change that, possibly by harming the outgroup.

Make the link

With the concept of identification in the topic of conformity and obedience.

Processes

There are four main processes described by social identity theory.

- **Social categorisation** – we mentally divide the social world into groups.
- **Social identification** – our sense of self is based on group membership such as job or nationality. This affects self-esteem.
- **Social comparison** – people like to compare groups. These comparisons are biased towards the ingroup, boosting self-esteem.
- **Psychological distinctiveness** – people like their groups to be distinctive from and superior to other groups, and will act to increase this.

The researchers also believed that a person's behaviour can switch between social identity and **personal identity**. In some situations, such as when talking to a close friend, our personal identity comes to the fore. In other situations, such as when playing a sports match with two teams in different colours, we focus more on social identity.

Evidence

People will begin to treat other people differently if they start to perceive them as outgroup members. There is evidence that people will form a sense of ingroup and outgroup on the basis of tiny differences, and will work to discriminate against the outgroup (Tajfel, 1970 – see Key study).

Judd and Park (1988) found that people evaluate outgroup members less favourably, and see them as being more alike in behaviour and appearance than members of the ingroup are.

Aim: The study aimed to find out what the minimum conditions are for discrimination to emerge.

Method: Schoolboys were shown 12 images of paintings by the modern artists Paul Klee and Wassily Kandinsky. The boys were then randomly allocated to a group, but were told that their choice of artwork was the reason behind the groupings.

Participants were then given the task of allocating small cash rewards to group members through filling in a booklet. They could pick from three options:

1. Maximum joint profit: the biggest overall reward to both groups.

2. Maximum ingroup profit: the best reward for the ingroup member.

3. Maximum difference: the amounts that caused the ingroup to be as far ahead of the outgroup as possible.

Findings: The responses favoured ingroup members, giving them higher rewards. Crucially though, rather than giving their ingroup the biggest rewards, the boys chose to create the biggest advantage of ingroup over the outgroup, regardless of the fact that this sometimes led to a lower reward for their own group. This is an example of psychological distinctiveness.

Evaluation: The task was highly artificial and short-term, therefore making it hard to generalise to real situations. Also, the participants were not representative of the population as a whole as they were all boys (although a great deal of other research into social identity has been conducted on other populations). Tajfel's experiment suggested that prejudice can't be explained in terms of conflict over limited resources – being the top group was found to be more important than getting more money. It therefore goes against realistic conflict theory (see the next section) and supports social identity theory.

Evaluation

Social identity is still a mainstream theory today. It has been successfully applied in a large number of areas, such as education.

However, its view of prejudice as being based on self-esteem may be over-simplistic. There are numerous other influences on self-esteem, not least a person's position within the group, as well as their individual achievements and image.

In addition, the concept doesn't entirely explain why interrelations between groups change over time.

Quick test

1. Name two processes from social identity theory.
2. Give a criticism of Tajfel's (1970) experiment.

🔑 Key concepts

- Social identity theory
- Social categorisation
- Social identification
- Social comparison
- Psychological distinctiveness
- Personal identity

Explanations of prejudice cont'd

Realistic conflict theory

Realistic conflict theory places an emphasis on situations where groups compete over limited resources. It states that prejudice is likely to occur when both sides cannot achieve their aims.

Evidence

The best-known evidence for realistic conflict theory comes from a series of studies that Muzafer Sherif and colleagues conducted on boys who were taken on summer camps and divided into groups. This research showed that conflict could easily be created, but also gave some insight into resolving it (see Key study).

📖 Key study: Sherif et al. (1954) – the Robber's Cave study

Aim: Sherif had conducted two previous summer camp studies examining conflict. This summary is based on the third published study where the key aim was to test realistic conflict theory and then to find ways to reduce conflict.

Method & Findings: The participants were 22 boys from Oklahoma City. They were similar to each other in background and schooling and none of them previously knew each other. They were divided into two matched groups of 11 and taken to the Robber's Cave National Park for their camp.

Week 1: the boys were kept separate, and the groups ('Eagles' and 'Rattlers') developed ingroup norms such as status, nicknames and favourite songs. In both groups a recognised 'leader' emerged. Each group was allowed to gradually discover that there was another group.

Week 2: a tournament between the groups was introduced. Name-calling began immediately after the groups met. An initial sense of 'good sportsmanship' broke down quickly, and fights began to occur. Both groups were asked to identify friends from the entire camp, and over 92% of choices came from the ingroup.

Week 3: Sherif and colleagues set out to replace the conflict with cooperation. Unstructured 'contact' situations simply led to fighting. The researchers then introduced superordinate goals via faked events that required all of the boys to work together to solve a problem. After working together, intergroup hostility dropped away.

Evaluation: The study had high ecological validity. It has great real-world relevance as a model for how to reduce prejudice. A limitation was that the sample were all boys, but similar examples of realistic conflict had also been demonstrated with girls. There were considerable ethical issues: participants were deceived, and put into several risky situations, while the conflict itself was highly stressful.

Evaluation

Realistic conflict theory provides an explanation for the reason behind prejudice (conflict over resources) and its resolution (**superordinate goals**), but both are rather absolute, and there are many real-world exceptions.

The evidence relating to the theory is mixed.

- The Robber's Cave study showed that prejudice easily developed, but this might have occurred even without conflict over resources.

- The Stanford prison experiment also quickly created inter-group hostility (Haney et al., 1973) in a position of unequal resources.
- Conflict over resources has been observed in real-world populations.
- However, not all conflicts involve limited resources.
- Tajfel (1970) showed that people prioritise group superiority, even when it meant that their group got less of a reward.

Scapegoat theory

Scapegoating is an extreme form of prejudice where an ingroup unfairly blames a specific outgroup, often an ethnic minority, for one or more social problems.

Evidence

Scapegoat theory links to a cognitive shortcut called **confirmation bias.** This is where people tend to notice information that fits their stereotypes, while ignoring information that goes against these stereotypes.

According to this idea, simplistic, stereotyped ideas about a group are activated by one or more incidents, such as member of an outgroup committing a crime. Confirmation bias would lead ingroup members to notice further examples that fit the stereotype, ignoring incidents that did not.

Scapegoat theory also fits with the idea that schemas about outgroup members tend to be simplistic. Brewer (1988) notes that people may begin with a 'prototype' schema of an outgroup member, and only form a more detailed schema after having multiple real-life opportunities to encounter the outgroup.

Evaluation

Scapegoat theory helps to highlight a serious and common problem – the targeting and blame of minorities by majority groups that feel threatened in some way.

However, scapegoat theory is a largely outdated idea of prejudice. It is no longer a current area of research, and tends to be seen as historical and over-simplistic.

Although it can describe a common problem, it can't fully explain why it happens. For example, it can't explain why some groups are scapegoated and not others, or the motivation for doing so. Such processes are more easily explained by realistic conflict theory and social identity theory.

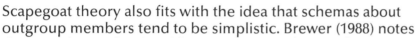

Quick test

1. According to realistic conflict theory, why do people dislike outgroup members?
2. What cognitive process could maintain and strengthen the process of scapegoating?

Key concepts

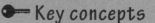

- Realistic conflict theory
- Superordinate goals
- Scapegoat theory
- Confirmation bias

Reducing prejudice

There are many programmes and interventions that have been used to reduce prejudice, and these fall into four main categories, as outlined below.

Top tip

When *analysing* strategies for reducing prejudice, link the strategies to theories and/or to real-world implications.

- **Education**: raising awareness of prejudice and its harmful effects.

- **Affirmative action**: the idea that prejudice will reduce if minority groups are given help to access privileged positions, thus tackling discrimination and increasing intergroup contact.

- **Superordinate goals**: creating situations where members of different groups have to work together to achieve a common goal.

- **Media**: films, TV and other media can either challenge or perpetuate stereotypes.

Education

Education involves tackling the cognitive aspect of intergroup bias. The main aims of education to reduce prejudice are:

- **raising awareness** about stereotypes

- teaching strategies to reduce prejudiced thinking.

Evidence

Jane Elliott was a teacher working in the USA at the time when civil rights leader Martin Luther King was assassinated. Elliott decided to tackle prejudice directly among the 3rd grade children she taught. She set up a scenario where children's eye colour would determine how they were treated.

- On day one, blue-eyed children in Elliott's class were told that they were social superiors.

- Blue-eyed children received privileges such as extra play time.

- Prejudice and name-calling spontaneously emerged.

- Brown-eyed children, having been labelled inferior, did worse at a card-sorting task.

- On the second day, the roles – and findings – were reversed.

Elliott's blue eyes–brown eyes exercise worked well with her all-white schoolchildren, but has not always been successful with more diverse groups.

It caused distress in the children, though most later said that they had found the process beneficial.

Education is the most common intervention against prejudice. It is widely conducted as part of the general social education curriculum. However, despite this, prejudiced attitudes are still widespread.

In adults, diversity training is a form of education aimed at reducing stereotypes, prejudice and discrimination. People are sometimes ordered to attend such courses after discriminatory or abusive behaviour.

Affirmative action

Affirmative action (also called 'positive action') is a political programme whereby in a similarly qualified pool of applicants for jobs or other positions, minority candidates are given preferential treatment. This is to balance out the discrimination and disadvantages they face, and also aims to make establishments more equal. It can include facilitating access for under-represented groups (for example, by providing help writing job applications). Such actions are legal in the UK, though only in situations where a minority is under-represented in the workforce.

According to Allport (1954), we are more likely to form stereotypes if we are ignorant of outgroups, while if we get to know them as individuals we will become less prejudiced. This idea is known as the **contact hypothesis**.

Allport thought that to be effective in reducing prejudice, individuals must cooperate on an equal basis without either group being superior or inferior. Affirmative action promotes equal status. In addition, increasing workforce equality provides role models for others, and could make the organisation more approachable to customers who are themselves from minorities.

Evidence

Laar et al. (2005) studied Dutch students who had been randomly allocated a roommate of a different race. After room sharing for several months, questionnaire data showed that participants became less prejudiced. However, it may not be possible to generalise from young students to other social groups. Also, the level of contact involved was much greater than is possible in most settings.

It is possible that a person employed via affirmative action could suffer some negative psychological effects. Brown et al. (2000) found that when women felt that they had been selected for their gender, their performance was worse in comparison to a random selection process, possibly due to stereotype threat.

Pettigrew and Martin (1987) argue that recipients of affirmative action suffer from 'triple jeopardy', three major negative effects:

- negative stereotypes within the organisation
- solo status – being the only member of the group, leading to increased stress
- token status – the sense that that they are only employed because of their characteristic, leading to unduly negative judgements by other employees.

Superordinate goals and the jigsaw technique

Having shared superordinate goals (see previous section) and having contact with other groups (as happens with affirmative action) can reduce prejudice. The **jigsaw technique** was developed to put these ideas into practice.

The key idea behind the jigsaw technique is that every member of a group must have an essential piece of information needed to complete the task (with the task itself being the superordinate goal). Each has one piece of the 'jigsaw', and everyone must be listened to because the task is impossible to complete without every piece. This promotes a respectful exchange of information.

Evidence

In the USA, after desegregation of schools, children from different races were finally in the same school classrooms. However, prejudice remained high. Aronson and Bridgeman (1979) used the jigsaw technique with elementary school pupils in Texas. After three weeks of this intervention, the researchers found improvements in several areas:

- self-esteem increased
- students reported higher liking for both ingroup and outgroup members
- academic performance increased
- there was less evidence of negative stereotypes of other ethnic groups.

The Sherif et al. (1954) study (see previous section) seems to suggest that contact alone is not enough. The Robber's Cave study involved a lot of contact, as does an everyday classroom situation in a school, but prejudice and stereotypes can remain strong. In the Sherif study in particular, there was no difference in status between the two groups of boys. This provides strong support for the importance of intergroup superordinate goals, and of using situations where conflicting groups are motivated to work together.

The media's role in prejudice

The **media** is able to either challenge or perpetuate stereotypes. Highly stereotyped roles on drama programmes or in books can boost levels of prejudice. Similarly, the language used in the media can be negative and stereotyped – many people have highlighted this in some sections of the press.

However, if the media can contribute to prejudice, there is also the potential to reduce it. Media campaigns can raise awareness of problems such as racism. An example is the 'Show Racism the Red Card' charity campaign, which used high-profile professional footballers to campaign against racism among fans and in schools.

Certain research studies have looked at the efficacy of interventions to reduce prejudice via the media (see below).

Evidence

Riggle et al. (1996) showed a video about the life of a homosexual politician, and questioned participants before, during and afterwards. The film reduced the level of prejudice. Such research is small-scale, however, and doesn't investigate the real-world timescales over which prejudice develops.

Paluck (2009) conducted a large-scale field study in Rwanda, which has experienced major problems with inter-group conflict, most notably the Rwandan genocide of 1994 during which one ethnic group mass-murdered another.

In Paluck's study, two versions of a radio soap opera were played for a year. The experimental group heard a version that portrayed an outgroup in positive ways, while the control group heard an informative health-based radio show. After one year, attitudes were tested.

- Attitudes towards social norms including inter-marriage with the outgroup had changed.
- However, participants' personal opinions showed fewer signs of change.

The findings suggest that the media can set the agenda in terms of what is seen as normal, but is less impactful in terms of privately held views.

The media's role in prejudice is still not fully understood, partly because it is difficult to conduct controlled experimentation.

It is also difficult to know whether prejudiced attitudes have changed because of the media, or if the media has changed because prevailing attitudes have changed.

Quick test

1. What physical feature did Elliott use as a model of prejudice?
2. What term is used to describe the type of goals that help to bring conflicting groups together?
3. What is diversity training?
4. Does affirmative action mean that jobs are given to people who are not fully qualified?
5. Briefly describe one example of how the media can challenge stereotypes.

🔑 Key concepts

- Education
- Raising awareness
- Elliott's blue eyes–brown eyes exercise
- Affirmative action
- Contact hypothesis
- Jigsaw technique
- Media

Social
relationships

7 Social relationships

Social exchange theory

! **Syllabus note**

This topic is in the Social Behaviour unit. Higher Psychology students must study Prejudice <u>or</u> Social Relationships <u>or</u> Aggression.

A **social relationship** means any ongoing attachment with another person. It can include friendships and family relationships, as well as our connections with acquaintances such as neighbours or even enemies. **Affiliation** is a broad term meaning the desire to form any such connections, which could occur for strategic reasons.

Social exchange theory (Thibaut and Kelley, 1959) suggests that social relationships can be looked at as a series of decisions. It explains each relationship in terms of people's **costs and benefits**. These could include:

Costs:

- time spent
- missing out on other options

Benefits:

- social support
- fun

Romantic relationships

Why do people form and maintain long-term **romantic relationships** with one another? Again, according to social exchange theory, this is largely a matter of weighing up costs and benefits, with each partner trying to get a good deal. Thibaut and Kelley also argued that everyone judges each relationship against a **comparison level** (CL), based on their schema for relationships. Each person's judgement will be slightly different based on their own experiences. This means that some may stay in a bad relationship despite the costs, because it exceeds their expectations.

Explanation of attraction

The **matching hypothesis** states that people will tend to select romantic partners of the same level of physical attractiveness as themselves. There is good evidence that this occurs – for example, real-life engaged couples are judged as more similar to one another in attractiveness than randomly-paired photographs (Murstein, 1972).

Matching can be explained in terms of costs and benefits – people wish to avoid costs such as time wasting and disappointment by aiming only as high as they can realistically achieve.

Aim: The researchers wanted to test the matching hypothesis – do people aim for partners of a similar level of attractiveness to themselves? According to social exchange theory, this is more likely to happen if there is a risk of rejection, which would be a cost.

Method: University students were invited to a 'computer matching dance', and were told that a computer would pick them a suitable date for the evening. Some were given an element of realistic risk, being told that the partner may refuse to continue with the date after an initial meeting, while others were not told this. Each participant was rated on a nine-point scale for physical attractiveness by four student accomplices, and participants also indicated how important certain factors were to them in a partner, including attractiveness, personality, intelligence, etc.

Findings: The researchers found evidence of matching, with participants rated higher on attraction also stating this as more important to them in their date. However, risk made no difference to the outcome – participants did not ask for less attractive dates even if they knew they could be rejected. This finding goes against social exchange theory.

Evaluation: The study used a large sample size and was well controlled, but the situation was still rather unrealistic, and might not reflect how people would normally behave.

Relationship stages

Costs and benefits can change as a relationship progresses. According to social exchange theory, this process leads to four key relationship stages:

- **sampling**: considering options and comparing other potential relationships
- **bargaining**: giving and receiving rewards such as gifts; trying to strike a good deal
- **commitment**: the relationship becomes more predictable, and so costs are lowered
- **institutionalisation**: norms are established, and things that were previously benefits become expectations.

Evaluation

Social exchange theory helps psychologists to explain how people choose among different options, and why many people stay in bad relationships.

The theory fits with the matching hypothesis, but struggles to explain the finding that a risk of rejection makes no difference to people's choices. It also doesn't fully explain what causes some people to be perceived as more attractive than others – this is better explained by evolutionary theories (see next section).

Overall it is rather unrealistic to reduce human relationships to a series of rational, strategic choices.

🔑 Key concepts

- Social relationship
- Affiliation
- Social exchange theory
- Attachment
- Romantic relationship
- Costs and benefits
- Comparison level
- Attraction
- Matching hypothesis
- Relationship stages: sampling, bargaining, commitment and institutionalisation

Quick test

1. What are the four stages in social exchange theory?
2. What is a comparison level?

Evolutionary theory

The **evolutionary theory of relationships** states that human relationship behaviour has been shaped by Darwinian natural selection – people engage in behaviour to maximise their reproductive success.

🔍 Top tip

When *analysing* theories in this topic, compare them with each other, using evidence and examples.

Parental investment

According to the evolutionary theory, males and females invest different amounts of resources in having and raising children, and this has led the two sexes to evolve different behavioural strategies (Trivers, 1972). Both parents have a genetic stake in a child's survival, but even in relatively equal societies, there are differences in the **parental investment** put in biologically:

- women bear the child through pregnancy
- only women breastfeed infants.

As with other species that have only one or two babies at a time and long pregnancies, women can have fewer offspring over the course of their life than men can. According to the theory, the following factors could affect behaviour.

- For females, the best evolutionary strategy in terms of gene survival would be to look after the offspring well and seek a supportive partner.

- Males could potentially have a larger number of offspring with many females, but doing so would mean less control over how well they are protected.

There are also similarities between the sexes. Both men and women will be motivated to avoid infidelity, but for different reasons. For a man, this is to ensure that he is not providing care for someone else's offspring. For a woman, this is because she would have to invest more effort if her children's father didn't stick around.

Dunbar's number

In contrast with theories that humans have evolved a large brain in order to do complex tasks, the **social brain hypothesis** states that our brains are large because we need to keep track of social relationships. Researcher Robin Dunbar states that the maximum number of people that we can know well (such that we know about their lives, who they are friends with, etc) is 150. This became known as **Dunbar's number**. The idea has been supported by the finding that a group size of around 150 seems to be fairly typical in humans through history, and the social group size of different primate species correlates with their brain size.

Innate factors

In research on monkeys, researcher Harlow (1959) found strong evidence that the way infants bond with their parents is largely **innate**, rather than being learned through rewards. Evolutionary theories of relationships also suggest that sexual attraction is innate, designed by evolution to maximise the chances of raising healthy offspring. According to this view, this leads to certain features being attractive:

- healthy skin tone
- facial symmetry (indicates a healthy immune system)
- average-sized facial features
- body shapes that indicate fertility.

Attraction may also be influenced by factors that we are unaware of. In a study that asked participants to rate the smell of body odour from t-shirts, Wedekind et al. (1995) found that romantic partner choice is partly based on **pheromones** (airborne hormones) that signal genetic compatibility, even though we aren't conscious of releasing or responding to these.

Evaluation

This theory is based on evolution by natural selection. It helps to explain aspects of relationships that do not seem to be based on rational choices, and gives more detail about why certain physical features are considered attractive.

However, it cannot easily explain same-sex relationships, because it states that relationships exist to pass on one's genes. The concept of parental investment tends to ignore the broader social context (e.g. the role played by friends/ family in a person's choice of partner), and can't fully explain why people choose to spend time and effort looking after children who they know are not related to them, for example foster children.

Another limitation of the evolutionary theory is that there are considerable cultural differences in what is considered attractive. If our relationship behaviour is innate and based around the evolutionary drive to pass on genes, it is hard to understand why it should be so easily influenced by culture.

Quick test

1. According to evolutionary theory, who is prone to jealousy – males, females or both?
2. Complete this sentence: Evolutionary theories of relationships focus on _____ investment.

🔑 Key concepts

- Evolutionary theory of relationships
- Parental investment
- Social brain hypothesis
- Dunbar's number
- Innate
- Pheromones

Filter theory and investment theory

Two further theories of relationships are **filter theory** and **investment theory**. Filter theory tries to connect the different factors that affect attraction, while investment theory gives a more realistic explanation of abusive relationships.

Filter theory

Filter theory examines the decisions that someone makes as they narrow the **field of potential partners** (Kerckhoff and Davis, 1962). It can be linked to the 'sampling' stage in social exchange theory, and provides an alternative to evolutionary theory.

The key idea is that decisions about partner choice pass through a series of filters, each of which narrows the range of options available. Some widely-discussed filters include the following.

- Availability: filter out anyone who is not eligible to be in a relationship.
- Category: filter by age and sexuality.
- Attractiveness: filter by physical appearance.
- Similarity: filter by social background and interests.
- Complementarity: filter on the basis of complementary views and preferences.
- Proximity: filter out people who do not live close by.

Evidence

Kerckhoff and Davis (1962) studied couples across the early stages of their relationships, and concluded that similarity acted as a filter prior to the effects of complementary views. This supports the idea that we use these filters one by one, with some (such as category and similarity) being active before others. Availability is the first filter to be used, according to this idea.

Brewer (1968) studied relationship choice in eastern Africa, and found that education level, proximity and perceived similarity all acted as filters.

Evaluation

This theory provides a useful explanation of the partner choice process. It fits with the 'sampling' phase of social exchange, and can complement some of the principles from evolutionary theories. However, it has several flaws:

- It does not fully explain why different people have different priorities.
- It is not clear which filter should take priority if they conflict.
- The concept of filtering out partners by proximity is outdated in an era where both travel and internet dating are common.
- The supporting research is dated, and focuses mainly on young heterosexual couples.

While filters seem to make some basic sense, there is relatively little evidence that people actually make choices on this basis. The findings conflict with evolutionary evidence of automatic attraction. Also, people do not always filter out potential partners on the basis of their availability (for example, see the discussion of parasocial relationships in the final section of this chapter).

Rusbult's investment theory

Caryl Rusbult's investment theory focuses particularly on whether and why relationships are maintained. The theory is based on the idea of **investment**. Rather than the evolutionary concept of parental investment (see previous section), Rusbult (1980) describes the psychological factors that make people feel that they have invested too much in a relationship for it to break up.

In addition to investment, two factors that affect relationship maintenance are as follows.

- Satisfaction level: is the person having their needs and wants met?

- Comparison with alternatives: do they have options besides their current relationship?

Rusbult also highlighted two elements that contribute to satisfaction.

- **Equity**: is what you put into a relationship proportional to what you get out?

- **Social network**: shared friends or strong family bonds.

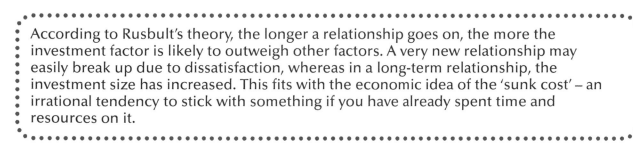

According to Rusbult's theory, the longer a relationship goes on, the more the investment factor is likely to outweigh other factors. A very new relationship may easily break up due to dissatisfaction, whereas in a long-term relationship, the investment size has increased. This fits with the economic idea of the 'sunk cost' – an irrational tendency to stick with something if you have already spent time and resources on it.

Evidence and evaluation

Compared to the ideas of costs, benefits and comparison levels Rusbult's idea of investment helps to explain why relationships may change over time.

Rusbult and Martz (1995) studied women in abusive relationships. They found greater levels of relationship commitment among those who:

- had few alternatives
- were less dissatisfied
- had already invested heavily in their relationships.

Rusbult's model can also be applied to explain same-sex relationships, giving it an advantage over evolutionary theories.

Key concepts

- Filter theory
- Field of potential partners
- Investment
- Equity
- Social network

Quick test

1. What is the first filter people use, according to the filter theory of romantic relationships?
2. What two elements contribute to relationship satisfaction, according to Rusbult?

Virtual relationships

Millions of people use the internet to form or maintain a social relationship, conducting the relationship partly or entirely online. Such relationships are called **virtual relationships** (or 'internet-mediated' relationships). Psychologists have become interested in whether virtual relationships share the same characteristics as traditional relationships.

Gating features

When forming a new relationship online, it's easier to overcome phenomena known as **gating features.** These include:

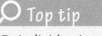

- shyness
- disabilities
- stigmatised aspects of appearance
- behavioural conditions such as stuttering.

Online, people can more easily present themselves the way they would like to be seen. This makes it easier for a broad range of people to form relationships, and also to express less conventional aspects of their identity (Suler, 2002).

Tosun and Lajunen (2010) found that students who were high in extraversion tended to use the internet to extend real-life relationships, whereas students who scored high on psychoticism tended to use the internet as a substitute for face-to-face relationships.

Reduced cues theory

What effect does online communication have on relationships? Sproull and Kiesler (1986) argued that without face-to-face social cues, people are likely to be rude and less willing to share. This became known as **reduced cues theory**.

> **Top tip**
>
> Deindividuation may affect the behaviour of online 'trolls' and bullies.

- Relative anonymity could mean that people don't fear consequences – a phenomenon called **deindividuation**.
- Where messages are relatively permanent, people might be unwilling to disclose their feelings.
- Reduced cues theory may be an over-simplification, as the amount people reveal depends on the context of the communication.

Walther's hyperpersonal theory

In contrast to reduced cues theory, Joseph Walther argued that the internet can improve communication (Walther, 1996). He suggested two key differences in such communication compared to face-to-face encounters.

- People can be strategic about what information they release.
- Communication may be asynchronous (messages may be read and responded to later, rather than at the time they were written).

According to Walther, this may make it easier for people to portray their **ideal self** rather than their true self online, and leads to deeper and more intimate communication – **hyperpersonal communication**. Its effects include:

- increased liking
- more intimate sharing of information
- in some cases, increased attraction to extreme views and values.

📖 Key study: Walther et al. (2018) – The effect of message persistence and disclosure on liking

Aim: The primary aim was to develop Walther's hyperpersonal theory, which suggests that online self-disclosures will lead to increased liking, rather than to weaker relationships because of reduced cues. The researchers thought the ability to read our own self-disclosure messages could affect the development of relationships.

Method: Participants – 136 undergraduate students – took part in a real-time text chat in pairs. Questions included 'intimate' topics. In one condition the participants' messages accumulated and remained visible, and in another condition they were invisible. The researchers also varied whether disclosures were reciprocated or whether partners deflected, saying neutral things like 'okay'. Participants then rated partners on a likeability questionnaire.

Findings: Message persistence didn't have an overall effect, but it interacted with reciprocal self-disclosures. When participants' own messages were visible and partners reciprocated, liking was high. The lowest level of liking was found when invisible messages were met with deflection.

Evaluation: The study supported the idea that the persistence of online messages can affect liking. A strength of the study is that the task had high mundane realism, although participants being told whether to disclose or not may have made it seem artificial. The participants were all undergraduates, making it hard to generalise to children or older adults.

Maintenance of existing relationships

As well as its role in relationship formation, the internet can make it much easier to maintain existing relationships. Kim and Lee (2011) found that greater honesty on Facebook tended to lead to more happiness and social support, and there is evidence that for people on the autism spectrum, online communication can be more accessible than its face-to-face equivalent.

Quick test

1. What are gating features?
2. True or false – people online are unwilling to share information with strangers according to Walther?.
3. What theory, devised by Sproull and Kiesler, describes the effect of a lack of face-to-face social cues when online?

🔑 Key concepts

- Virtual relationships
- Gating features
- Hyperpersonal communication
- Ideal self
- Deindividuation
- Reduced cues theory

Parasocial relationships

A **parasocial relationship** is an intense one-sided relationship between an ordinary individual and a celebrity. The individuals may feel as if they know the celebrity, and often research them in a huge amount of detail. It may be perceived by others as a crush or obsession.

Some features of parasocial relationships are outlined below.

- They are commonly found among adolescents.
- They are more likely to occur when the celebrity and fan have similar values.
- Celebrities can provide positive role models for people to emulate.
- However, attempts to emulate celebrities can lead to eating disorders, or harm self-esteem.
- There is a link between more intense parasocial relationships and poorer mental health.

Levels of parasocial relationships

Giles and Maltby (2006) identified three levels of parasocial relationships.

- **Entertainment-social:** the fan enjoys keeping up with news and gossip about the celebrity, and discussing them with friends – or anyone else who will listen.
- **Intense-personal:** the fan has developed a level of obsession towards the celebrity. They may react to problems experienced by the celebrity as strongly as if it had happened to them or to a family member.
- **Borderline pathological:** beliefs about the celebrity show clear signs of being out of touch with reality, and emotions are at the extreme end of the scale. The fan may express a willingness to die for the celebrity.

These levels mirror the three dimensions of **Eysenck's personality theory**:

- extraversion
- neuroticism
- psychoticism

People may therefore experience all levels to different degrees, and the level that someone is at may reflect their personality, rather than there being a gradual progression towards more extreme levels.

Sheridan et al. (2006) have suggested a fourth level – active attempts by the fan to make contact, accompanied by delusional beliefs that they have a real relationship with the celebrity. According to some definitions, this is **stalking**.

> ### 🔍 Top tip
> If asked to analyse theories or explanations in this topic, gain marks by identifying the aims of each theory, and comparing them to each other.

Attachment theory

Ainsworth et al. (1971) presented three **types of attachment** in child–parent relationships:

- secure: the child is distressed on separation but happy to be reunited

- insecure-avoidant: the child is unaffected by separation

- insecure-resistant: the child is distressed on separation and angry when reunited.

Hazan and Shaver (1987) stated that a similar pattern can occur in romantic relationships. An insecure-resistant attachment could lead to clingy and obsessive behaviour, and being highly upset by rejection.

Someone who tends to have insecure-resistant attachments may prefer a parasocial relationship. In this context they cannot be rejected, and can act in an obsessive way without consequence.

Parasocial relationships could therefore be connected to an individual's other attachments, including those from childhood. Giles and Maltby (2004) found that an intense interest in celebrities was connected to low levels of closeness to parents.

Absorption is an extreme focus that results in the celebrity coming before all else in the individual's thoughts. This obsessional focus may serve to fill emotional gaps, meaning that the pleasure the person gains from their obsessive behaviour may have an **addictive** quality. Like other addictions, the person may develop a level of tolerance, helping to explain why some progress to increasingly high levels of celebrity worship and can experience psychological withdrawal if denied access to a means of following the object of their focus. Together, these concepts make up the **absorption–addiction** model (McCutcheon et al., 2002).

Key concepts

- Parasocial relationship
- Levels of parasocial relationships
- Entertainment-social
- Intense-personal
- Borderline pathological
- Eysenck's personality theory
- Stalking
- Types of attachment
- Absorption–addiction model

Quick test

1. At which level of parasocial relationships would a person appear to be out of touch with reality?

2. Which of Ainsworth's types of attachment links to behaviour in parasocial relationships, and why?

3. What similarity does a parasocial relationship have with addiction?

Aggression

8 Aggression

Aggression is an area of social psychology. One possible definition of aggression is that it includes any deliberate harmful act towards another member of the same species. Some definitions also include emotions, but this is less objective because it is not always possible to know what people or animals are feeling when they behave aggressively. In addition, only certain types of aggression involve emotions such as anger.

Four different types of aggression are outlined below.

- **Impulsive:** a spontaneous harmful or violent act, such as hitting someone or saying something unpleasant about them.

- **Instrumental:** a harmful act that aims to advance a person's goals or gain something for them, such as stealing.

- **Sanctioned:** a harmful act that is within the rules of a society, such as executing a criminal.

- **Passive:** an act that causes harm or upset by being uncooperative without being overtly aggressive, such as not talking to people or deliberately doing tasks badly.

Biological influences on aggression

Hormonal influences

A hormone is a chemical messenger that travels round the bloodstream affecting organs or other parts of the body. One hormone that plays a role in aggression is **testosterone**, a male sex hormone that is also produced by women's bodies at lower levels. Behavioural effects of testosterone include:

- high levels link to more intense competitive behaviour

- males with higher levels of testosterone have more sexual partners

- raised levels are associated with increased fighting in many species.

Birds have increased levels of testosterone when they are fighting for territory. Animals have also shown increased aggression when injected with testosterone, but its effects in humans are less clear cut. Explaining aggression in terms of testosterone levels helps to explain why men are responsible for more violent crimes than women, but other factors must also be involved.

The **challenge hypothesis** states that testosterone causes animals to seek and retain mates. This could involve fighting off challengers and trying to keep mates that they have already paired up with – behaviour known as '**mate-guarding**'.

Neural influences

Another biological factor in aggression is the role of particular brain areas. The **limbic system** is a set of brain structures closely linked to the frontal lobe of the neocortex, and is involved in emotion. Within it is an area called the **amygdala** that processes fear and aggression.

Stimulating the amygdala with electrodes can prompt aggressive behaviour. There have also been cases where individuals with abnormalities in the amygdala have engaged in aggressive behaviour. Raine et al. (1997) found that brain scans of murderers showed less activity in the frontal lobe as well as in the corpus callosum, the fibres that connect the two sides of the brain. However, it is hard to explain everyday aggressive acts in terms of brain abnormalities.

The neurotransmitter serotonin may also affect aggression. Normal levels of this neurotransmitter are important for healthy calm mood; Brown et al. (1979) studied navy recruits and found that low levels of serotonin linked to higher impulsive aggression. However, abnormally high levels of serotonin can also link to aggression.

Genetic influences

Some people are more aggressive than others, and genetic explanations for this have focused on the different versions of a gene called monoamine oxidase A (abbreviated to **MAOA**). One version of this gene, MAOA-L, leads to higher levels of serotonin and other monoamine neurotransmitters, potentially influencing mood and aggression (see above).

Make the link

With the role of MAOA and the diathesis-stress model in the topic of Depression.

In a study of men who had suffered abuse as children, Caspi et al. (2002) found that around 12% of participants had the MAOA-L gene, but that they were responsible for almost half of the convictions for violent crimes in the sample. This supports the idea that some biological differences in aggression may have a genetic cause, but life events play a role too.

Epigenetics is the process of genes being switched off or on depending on the environment, meaning that two people with the same gene might not show the same behaviour. A baby's exposure to testosterone is one environmental factor that could interact with genes. Male foetuses who are exposed to more testosterone may become more aggressive as adults, but this process is still not fully understood.

Key concepts

- Aggression
- Impulsive aggression
- Instrumental aggression
- Sanctioned aggression
- Passive aggression
- Testosterone
- Mate-guarding
- Limbic system
- Amygdala
- MAOA
- Epigenetics

Quick test

1. What type of aggression is involved if a gang leader persuades a gang member to rob someone?
2. In which part of the brain is the amygdala?
3. Give an example of an environmental factor that could lead to a gene being switched on or off.

Evolutionary and ethological explanations

Evolutionary and ethological explanations both attempt to explain aggression in terms of how biological processes interact with the environment.

Evolutionary explanations

Evolutionary psychology is the application of Darwin's theory of natural selection as it applies to human behaviour. According to this approach, aggression derives from strategies that helped our ancestors to survive and reproduce. Evolutionary psychologists have compared our behaviour with aggression in other primates.

- Some species show high levels of aggression among males and have very unequal breeding rights, with a 'dominant' male. Males in such species are much larger than females.

- Other species show much lower levels of aggression. Males and females form pair bonds and raise offspring relatively equally, and look very similar to one another.

Humans may have used elements of both strategies through our evolution. We are also a highly social species, and instrumental aggression, including gossip, can link to trying to establish a better place within a **social hierarchy**.

Ethology

While evolutionary psychology focuses on mating strategies and survival in humans, ethology places more of an emphasis on the natural habitat, and studies animals that are not particularly closely related to humans. Two key concepts from ethology are outlined below.

- A **fixed action pattern**: a set of behaviours that is partly innate and automatic but can adapt to specific environmental contexts. For example, a squirrel burying nuts.

- A **releaser**: these are situations or social cues ('**social releasers**') that prompt an individual to perform a fixed action pattern. For example, a baby bird opening its beak prompts a parent bird to feed it.

Three European researchers developed ethology: Niko Tinbergen, Karl von Frisch and Konrad Lorenz. All three conducted numerous studies of different animal species. Many of the studies were carried out in natural surroundings.

- von Frisch investigated how bees communicate about nectar sources via a 'waggle dance' in the hive.

- Lorenz showed how newly hatched geese 'imprint' to form a permanent bond with their mother. He also noted that most animals have releasers that bring a fight to an end, and argued that humans may have lost this trait.

- Tinbergen is known for his studies of aggression over mating and **territory** in fish and birds, including a classic study of stickleback fish (see Key study).

Key study: Tinbergen's (1952) study of aggression in sticklebacks

Aim: The study aimed to explore courtship and aggression in stickleback fish. They wanted to find social releasers that prompt aggressive behaviour.

Method: At mating time, male sticklebacks build a nest in the sand and attempt to drive out intruders by showing their bright red scales. Tinbergen tested this by putting two males close together, and by using model fish of various colours.

Findings: A male stickleback would treat most model fish as if they were a rival male, but showed the most aggression towards red models. Real males did very little real fighting, and instead made jerky movements towards each other. The researchers concluded that their aggression is largely a form of ritual. The researchers also found that a female will attempt to follow a red model fish even if there is no nest, but only when they were pregnant.

Evaluation: Tinbergen believed that the concepts of territory and ritualised aggression generalised to humans, but in reality it is likely that human aggression is more complex. The study provided objective evidence of how biological drives such as hormones interact with social and environmental stimuli. As a lab experiment, the study was well controlled, though some aspects caused harm to the fish.

Top tip

Several areas fall under the heading of biological explanations of aggression: neural and hormonal, genetic, evolutionary, and ethological. If asked to explain research into a biological explanation of aggression, you can focus on a study from any of these areas. For example, Tinbergen's ethological research would be acceptable.

Key concepts

- Evolution
- Social hierarchy
- Fixed action pattern
- Releaser
- Social releaser
- Territory

Quick test

1. Why is aggression thought to have evolved?
2. What is a social releaser?

Social learning theory

While it is generally accepted that brain areas and hormones play a role in aggression, several theories focus more on the social and **cognitive** processes that lead to aggression in particular contexts. One of these is **social learning theory.**

Social learning theory has elements of two major approaches to psychology.

- Like the **behaviourist** approach to psychology, social learning theory explains behaviour primarily in terms of learning.
- Like the cognitive approach, it recognises that people make mental models of actions and their outcomes.

In combination, this means that people learn not just from their own actions, but from those of others, particularly actions that they see being rewarded. This is known as **observational learning**. A major area of research is the work of Bandura and colleagues. These researchers developed social learning theory, and studied learning of aggression by children who observe adult violence.

Bobo doll studies

Bandura and colleagues conducted several studies to test their theory. Many of these studies involved an adult attacking a large inflatable toy doll, known as a **Bobo doll**. Children would watch this live or via a recording on TV, and would then be given a chance to play in a room including both the doll and various other toys. One study created a 'cartoon' version where the scene was made to look unrealistic and the adult was dressed up as a cat (see Key study).

The main findings of these studies were that children:

- were more likely to imitate aggression from an adult of their own sex
- were more likely to imitate aggression seen live rather than on a screen, though the difference was small
- were more likely to imitate realistic violence, though the difference was small
- would imitate specific aspects of aggression, such as the use of a weapon
- would imitate verbal aggression
- were more likely to imitate aggression if it was seen to be rewarded.

Aim: The study aimed to find out whether TV and movie violence was potentially harmful to children by measuring whether they would remember and repeat adult violence that they had watched.

Method: The researchers studied 96 preschool children in groups that had been matched according to prior aggression scores as judged by nursery teachers. In the aggressive live model condition, children saw the adult attack the Bobo doll by punching him, hitting him with a mallet, and yelling things like 'kick him'. The aggressive film condition was essentially the same, but the violence was shown to children via a TV screen. The 'cartoon' condition featured the same violence, again via a TV, but with the model dressed in a cat costume ('Herman the cat'), background music, and unrealistic-looking coloured surroundings.

All children including a control group then had attractive toys taken away from them in order to prompt frustration, and finally were given a chance to play with the Bobo doll and were watched by three observers.

Findings: Overall there were more violent acts from participants following the live aggression condition than the other groups, but the difference was slight. There were around three times as many violent acts from those in the cartoon condition than the control group. There were also some gender differences: boys were more aggressive overall, and particularly so if the role model was male. Females imitated verbal aggression more from a female model than a male. Researchers concluded that witnessing violent acts can lead to repetition of those acts, even by young children.

Evaluation: There were major ethical issues with deliberately exposing young children to violence, as later imitation could have harmed their classmates or siblings. A strength of the study was its use of more than one observer, and the ratings of these observers were found to be very similar.

Quick test

1. What term means learning from others rather than through your own experience?
2. Which gender showed more aggression in Bandura et al.'s study?
3. How did Bandura et al. make the aggression in the 'cartoon' condition appear less realistic? Mention two things.

🔑 Key concepts

- Behaviourist
- Cognitive
- Social learning theory
- Observational learning
- Bobo doll

Theories of violence in institutions

Psychologists have tried to explain why aggression occurs in prisons, for example rioting, attacks on prison guards, or abuse by the guards themselves. Three key explanations are Sykes' deprivation model, the importation model and the concept of dysfunctional institutions.

The deprivation model

Sykes (1958) believed that rather than prison violence occurring because prisoners are bad people, they are frustrated by being deprived of the key needs and wants of life. This is known as the **deprivation model** of aggression.

There are five key things that prisoners are deprived of, according to this model.

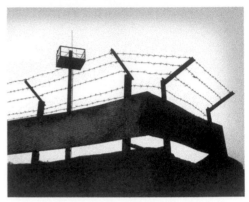

- Liberty: prisoners are not free to go where they please.

- Goods: prisoners are not free to buy things that would make their lives better.

- Relationships: prisoners don't have freedom to maintain sexual relationships.

- Autonomy: prisoners can't choose how to spend their time.

- Security: prisoners often don't feel safe.

This model is based on the idea that frustration leads to aggression: the **frustration–aggression hypothesis** (Dollard et al., 1939) – an idea that was largely accepted at the time, but has since come to be viewed as over-simplistic.

A problem with the theory is that deprivation is not an absolute condition. Instead, people judge deprivation relative to other groups and to their expectations. A sense of unfairness can lead to aggression, even if one's group is objectively better off than others.

This theory also struggles to explain why aggression levels are different in different prisons.

The importation model

Irwin and Cressey (1962) suggested that prisoners bring violent habits and social norms into an institution when they are imprisoned. This idea is known as the **importation model** of aggression. They argued that three sub-cultures can be seen in prisons.

- **Thief sub-culture** is the dominant sub-culture for most criminals outside of prison. It features loyalty and a disregard for society's rules.

- **Convict sub-culture** is the dominant sub-culture within the prison. It has similarities to gang culture, and features tough and manipulative behaviour.

- **Legitimate sub-culture** is the dominant sub-culture for people who had had little previous experience of criminality. It features low levels of aggression, at least initially.

Prisoners from the thief sub-culture are mainly interested in getting out, but may engage in prison violence through a sense of loyalty to the group. Convict sub-culture is more overtly aggressive in order to assert status, and such prisoners will be violent if frustrated from attaining their goals.

The importation model fits with other explanations of how society and culture affect behaviour. However, Gravel et al. (2013) found that the strategy of separating gang members inside prison had some inconsistent effects. Ekland-Olson et al. (1983) found that the main factor affecting prison violence was the age of the prisoners – younger prisoners committed more aggressive acts. This doesn't fit well with the importation theory, and even less so with the deprivation model.

Dysfunctional institutions

Philip Zimbardo and colleagues believed that **dysfunctional institutions** – places separated from the outside world, with a harmful set of values and social norms that were difficult to scrutinise or challenge – can lead to aggression by guards as well as prisoners. They conducted a study based in a mock prison. Student volunteers were randomly allocated to the role of prisoner or guard. Participants adopted the expectations of their assigned roles, with the guards becoming increasingly abusive.

The study showed a model of a dysfunctional institution, as there was no mechanism for changing the approach of the institution. The researchers argued that in the real world, violence is not due to personality, sub-culture or deprivation but because people adapt to the expectations of their social role (Haney et al., 1973), a process that they termed **situational attribution**.

However, later researchers have argued that Zimbardo's prison experiment was biased because the researchers' instructions prompted guards to act in an abusive way.

> ### 🔍 Top tip
>
> A social norm is a behaviour that is widely accepted in a particular group or culture, but that is not inevitable and may change over time.

> ### 🔑 Key concepts
>
> - Deprivation model
> - Frustration–aggression hypothesis
> - Importation model
> - Thief sub-culture
> - Convict sub-culture
> - Legitimate sub-culture
> - Dysfunctional institutions
> - Situational attribution

Quick test

1. Which sub-culture was most strongly associated with aggression, according to the importation model?
2. What term did Zimbardo and colleagues use for the way people adapt to the expectations of their role in a dysfunctional institution?

Media influences on aggression

How do media affect children? Is it possible that children learn aggression from TV or computer games?

Cognitive priming and television

Cognitive priming is the idea that watching a stimulus may affect later responses without our awareness. Media violence may cause people to learn an aggressive schema (or '**script**' – a term meaning a schema for a social situation), leading to aggressive responses in future situations.

Bushman (1998) showed people movie clips, one violent and one non-violent, and then gave them a word association task. Participants were more likely to make violence-related word associations after watching the violent clip.

The Bandura et al. (1963) study is also an example of how children's prior observation can affect later behaviour, and therefore links to cognitive priming.

Two real-world cases about the availability of television provide evidence about cognitive priming:

- In the island of St Helena, television was introduced in 1995, and researchers concluded that it made little difference to children's aggression (Charlton, 1998).

- Williams (1986) studied the introduction of television to towns in a region of Canada, and found increased levels of aggression among children who received TV, as well as reduced IQ and fewer child–adult interactions.

It is difficult to generalise from these studies as each location had unique features. It is likely that exposure to media violence interacts with other factors such as local culture and parenting.

Disinhibition

Even when people are motivated to be aggressive, they can be inhibited from acting. This means they do not actually carry out aggressive actions due to their identity or fears of how others will react.

Disinhibition means that this inhibition is reduced in situations where we are anonymous, such as riots that take place at night. Disinhibition has been linked with:

- antisocial behaviour in crowds
- more crime in conditions of darkness.

Disinhibition can also lead to increased obedience to harmful commands. Behaviour online can be more anonymous than in most real-world interactions, and this may contribute to the unpleasant behaviour of 'trolls'. Four factors contribute to this behaviour (Suler, 2004).

- Invisibility: the online trolls can't be seen or identified.
- Asynchronicity: there is often no immediate negative reaction.
- Dissociative imagination: the trolls often adopt an alternate identity.
- Lack of authority: no authority figures with the power to punish bad behaviour.

Computer games

Playing **violent computer games** has been linked with aggression, but it has been hard for researchers to establish a cause-and-effect relationship. Some of the key evidence is outlined below.

🔍 **Top tip**

When *analysing* media influences on aggression, compare these different explanations with each other.

- Anderson and Dill (2000) found that participants who had played a violent game acted more aggressively in a later task (see Key study).

- Playing violent games cooperatively can offset their effects on players' aggression levels (Velez et al., 2016).

- Durkin and Barber (2002) found that 16-year-old gamers were as well-adjusted as their peers, and no more prone to risky behaviour, and gamers have also been found to score favourably on school engagement and mental health.

- Ferguson (2014) argued that computer games studied may differ on variables besides violence, such as their level of difficulty. This could lead to confounding variables in the research.

📖 Key study: Anderson and Dill's (2000) study of violent video games

Aim: The researchers aimed to test the effect of video game violence using a laboratory experiment to rule out pre-existing differences between groups (the idea that aggressive people are drawn to games, rather than the games making people aggressive).

Method: Over 200 Psychology students played either a violent or a non-violent video game for 30 minutes. One week later they played a competitive task during which they could 'punish' an opponent by playing a blast of noise (no such punishments were actually given).

Findings: Participants who had previously played the violent game gave longer blasts of noise. The researchers concluded that the violent game increased aggression via cognitive priming. Females gave slightly more severe punishments than males.

Evaluation: The study was replicable and well controlled, but participants may have guessed the aim and altered their behaviour accordingly. The differences in punishments were small in real terms, and the study lacked mundane realism.

Quick test

1. Which explanation, cognitive priming or disinhibition, suggests that people are more aggressive because they are less affected by the consequences of their actions?

2. Compare two studies that investigated the first introduction of television to a part of the world.

🔑 Key concepts

- Cognitive priming
- Script
- Disinhibition
- Violent computer games

Research

This chapter explains the key scientific principles that you need to understand both for your own psychology research and when tackling exam questions.

Ethical and scientific standards

All research in psychology aims to provide good quality data that aids our understanding of human behaviour. In doing so, it must follow practices that ensure data are accurate and unbiased, while maintaining ethical standards – principles that mean research participants are treated fairly and protected from harm or distress.

Sampling

Sampling means selecting participants from the **target population**. A good sample will be large, and unbiased. It should contain the same variety of people as found among the people who the researcher is interested in studying – in other words, it should be **representative** of the target population as a whole.

Random sampling

A **random** sample is where every individual in a population has an equal chance of being chosen. This could be done by drawing names from a hat, or allocating computer-generated random numbers to each member of the population. Random sampling usually results in a representative sample, but is time-consuming to carry out.

Opportunity sampling

An **opportunity** sample is chosen on the basis of convenience, for example by asking members of your class to take part. This is usually the easiest sampling method but suffers from bias – some members of the population will be under-represented.

Volunteer sampling

A **volunteer** sample (or 'self-selecting sample') means that participants come forward of their own choice, perhaps responding to an advert. It is simple to arrange, but the sample may be biased towards outgoing members of the population.

Systematic sampling

A **systematic** sample involves regular selection of participants from a list, such as every 20th name from a school register. It is preferable to opportunity sampling, but can be biased depending on the nature of the list used.

> For any type of sampling, limits can be placed on the number of participants gathered from particular groups. For example, an all-female group could be selected, with potential male participants immediately rejected. This is called setting a **quota**. If the quota aims to be in line with the proportions of the population as a whole (for example, the sample is limited to 50% male and 50% female), then it is described as a **stratified** sample.

Research ethics

Researchers must follow a set of moral principles known as a **code of ethics,** which states what is and is not acceptable in research. Such codes are published by professional organisations such as the **BPS** (British Psychology Society).

Consent and briefing

Participants should give **informed consent**; consent means that they agree to take part in full knowledge of what they are agreeing to. A briefing should be given, explaining what the study will entail. Participants must also be debriefed, meaning that after the study has taken place, all relevant aspects are explained to them.

Right to withdraw

Participants have the **right to withdraw** from any study at any time, and may retrospectively withdraw consent when the study is over, in which case their data must be destroyed.

Avoiding harm

There should be no **harm** to participants, physical or mental. Their psychological well-being, health and dignity should be protected, and any risk of harm must be no greater than in ordinary life.

Confidentiality

Confidentiality should be maintained. This means that results should be kept secure, and when they are published, no names or identifying information should be included.

Research on children

Student researchers must not carry out experiments on children, and professional researchers take particular care to avoid harm and distress. Children must be willing to take part, and parental consent must be given on their behalf by a parent or carer.

Deception

Deception is where participants have been deliberately misled about the nature or purposes of a study, such as in Milgram's (1963) study of obedience. Student researchers should avoid deceiving participants; when commenting on classic studies, consider how severe the deception was and whether there was any reasonable alternative.

> **Top tip**
>
> As described in the Exam Skills chapter, ethical issues are relevant to most evaluation questions. Look for any obvious ethical flaws such as deception or psychological harm, and if the study was well run or notably better than previous studies, then the strength of its ethics can be commented on.

Quick test

1. Complete the following sentence:

   In a true random sample, every member of the target population has an _____ chance of being selected.

2. Look at the example below. Which sampling method is being used?

   > Two researchers decide to select participants for a lab experiment in a school setting. They place adverts on a main school noticeboard, announcing that the testing will be taking place every lunchtime that week, and that anyone over the age of 16 is welcome to participate. They also offer a free cup of tea and a biscuit for anyone who takes part.

Key concepts

- Sampling
- Target population
- Representative
- Random
- Opportunity
- Volunteer
- Systematic
- Quota
- Stratified
- Code of ethics
- BPS (British Psychology Society)
- Informed consent
- Right to withdraw
- Harm
- Confidentiality

Experiments and variables

The IV and DV

As you will see throughout the course, experiments play a huge role in psychology. This is because the experiment is a highly controlled research method, allowing variables to be manipulated so that researchers can determine whether one variable has an effect on the other. Experiments therefore aim to study **cause and effect**.

A variable can be any aspect of behaviour (such as heart rate), or any stimulus that affects behaviour (such as noise). The two key variables in any experiment are:

- the IV – **independent variable** (the variable the experimenter changes)
- the DV – **dependent variable** (the variable the experimenter measures)

The IV is always the predicted cause and the DV is always the effect. So, if you could put the key research variables into a sentence like '__ is causing __ to change' or 'Does __ have an effect on __?' then the first one in the sentence would be the IV, the second would be the DV.

If you put the results in a classic bar graph, the IV is typically along the bottom, its conditions shown in the names of two (or more) bars, and the DV is shown up the y-axis, with the height of the bar indicating the score on the DV.

Hypotheses

Experiments and other studies set out a **hypothesis** at the start. This is a scientific prediction of what the researchers expect to find, based on past research and theories.

In an experiment, the experimental hypothesis states that the IV will have an effect on the DV. More specifically, it could state that the IV will increase the DV or that it will decrease the DV. For example:

> **Top tip**
>
> Remember that identifying the IV and DV only really applies to experiments – for things like case studies, there typically won't be a single pair of variables.

- A high level of stress will decrease a person's score on a test of working memory.

Often, a null hypothesis is also stated. This simply says what the results will look like if the IV does not affect the DV. The researchers can then clearly state which hypothesis (experimental or null) has been supported by the findings.

Conditions of the IV

An experiment has at least two parts, known as **experimental conditions**. Each condition involves a group of people who experience a particular level of the IV. The conditions are therefore determined by whatever aspect of the IV researchers are trying to investigate. There must be at least two conditions of the IV in order to make a comparison. If one of the conditions represents 'no change' to participants' normal experience, this is called a control group.

For example, in Czeisler's study of sleep and shift work, the IV was whether participants were exposed to bright light or not. One group of participants were exposed to extremely bright lighting (bright light condition), and others to normal artificial light (dim light/control condition). This allowed Cziesler and his colleagues to measure the effect on people's sleep timing (the DV), thereby showing a cause and effect relationship.

In some cases, the people in the two conditions are two separate groups (an 'independent groups' design), and in other cases it might be preferable to test the same people for both/all conditions (a 'repeated measures' design).

Other variables

Outside variables that may cause random errors in results are called **extraneous variables**. These include environmental variables such as background noise, as well as participant variables (differences between participants, such as their abilities).

If an extraneous variable influences one condition more than the other, it is called a confounding variable. It then becomes difficult or impossible to know what causes a change in the results – the IV, or the confounding variable.

A true experiment randomly allocates participants to experimental conditions. If a repeated measures design is used, the order in which they do the conditions is randomised. **Random allocation** is used because it helps researchers to avoid confounding variables. If the experimental groups used were not randomly chosen, there could be pre-existing differences between the groups of participants, or the choice of participants for each group might be biased.

Imagine you are going to run a problem-solving test on two groups of school pupils as part of your Assignment, and decided to use two Higher History classes from your school. There may be important differences between those two classes. For example, perhaps one class chose History in that column to avoid doing Higher Maths, because they are bad at maths. That group might do worse on your problem-solving test if it involves some number work. This would lead to a confounding variable in your research.

Key concepts

- Cause and effect
- IV – independent variable
- DV – dependent variable
- Hypothesis
- Experimental conditions
- Extraneous variables
- Random allocation

Quick test

1. Complete the following sentences.
   a) The variable that a researcher manipulates is called the _____ variable.
   b) The variable that is measured is called the _____ variable.

2. What prediction made at the outset of an experiment assumes that the IV will <u>not</u> have an effect on the DV?

3. Look at the scenario below and answer the questions that follow.

   A sports psychologist wants to study the effect of hours of practice on football players' ability to score penalties. The researcher thinks that only specific penalties practice will lead to improvements in players' ability to take penalties. She obtains a sample of players from a local sports club, and allocates players to two experimental groups. One does an extra 30 minutes per day of general shooting practice for one week. The other group does an extra 30 minutes of specific penalties practice per day for a week.

   a) What was the IV in this study?
   b) Explain what the DV of the study would be, and how the researcher would measure it.
   c) State a possible experimental hypothesis for the study.
   d) Do you think that this study should have used a control group? Explain your answer.

4. What term means the different parts of an experiment that link to different values of an independent variable?

5. Explain why an experiment can demonstrate a cause-and-effect relationship.

Types of experiment

Ecological validity

There are several types of experiment. A key factor that affects a researcher's choice of experiment type is **ecological validity**. This essentially means how realistic the context of the study is.

A study that takes place in a participant's natural environment and involves a realistic task is said to have high ecological validity. This means that it is true to life (not artificial). This often makes it easier to generalise the conclusions of the study to behaviour in everyday life.

However, there may be a trade-off between realism and control, with more tightly controlled studies having lower ecological validity.

Laboratory and field experiments

Experiments may be conducted in a laboratory ('in the lab') or in the 'field':

- **lab experiment** – conducted in any controlled, artificial environment

- **field experiment** – conducted in the participants' natural environment, such as their home or workplace.

An advantage of lab experiments is that potential extraneous variables from the surroundings, such as noise, are controlled, reducing random error. They also provide researchers with easy access to equipment that might be hard to move around, such as the apparatus used in a sleep lab. Their major disadvantage is that being in an artificial environment, they lack ecological validity – participants may not behave in a natural way. The field experiment is the opposite – ecological validity is high, but environmental variables are not controlled.

Milgram's obedience study (see 'Conformity and Obedience' chapter) was an example of a lab experiment. It kept a high level of control, but the artificial lab environment makes it harder to know the level of obedience would be similar in a more everyday situation. Hofling et al. (1966) addressed this problem by carrying out a study of obedience on nurses in a hospital ward. As it took place in a normal workplace, their field experiment was high in ecological validity.

Other types of experiment

A **quasi-experiment** (meaning: 'partial experiment') may control the setting and procedure of a study, but it does not have control over the IV. The IV is usually something fixed such as a participant's sex or personality. In the topic of Stress (see chapter 4), Friedman and Rosenman's study of Type A and Type B behaviour is a quasi-experiment, as participants already had those characteristics – they weren't randomly allocated to experimental groups. Clearly it would also be impossible to randomly allocate to groups if the IV under investigation was male vs. female.

A **natural experiment** is not controlled by a researcher at all, but the structure resembles an experiment. For example, a researcher might look at two popular study strategies, and compare their effect on people's exam results. It is possible to treat study strategies like an IV and the exam results like a DV, but it is also important to remember that with no control and no random allocation, this is not a true experiment and confounding variables cannot be ruled out. Another example, also from the topic of Stress, is Nuckolls et al.'s (1972) study of pregnant women. They compared women under high stress vs. women under low stress to find the health outcomes. This is a form of IV and DV, but for obvious ethical reasons, the researchers didn't put the women under stress. Instead, the stress was occurring (or not occurring) by itself, and for this reason the study was a natural experiment.

Quick test

1. Researchers decide to conduct a lab experiment studying dating. What level of ecological validity might this study have, and why would this be a problem in terms of the strength of their conclusions?

2. Researchers conduct a study that compares the aggression levels of people who typically shop online versus people who typically go to shopping centres. Explain how this could be conducted either as a quasi- or natural experiment.

Key concepts

- Ecological validity
- Lab experiment
- Field experiment
- Quasi-experiment
- Natural experiment

Non-experimental methods

For various reasons, it might be impractical for a researcher to run an experiment. They may wish to investigate something that is impossible to manipulate or to measure directly, such as brain damage or people's beliefs about the effect of traumatic experiences. In such situations, researchers make use of **non-experimental methods** such as interviews, case studies and questionnaire surveys.

Questionnaire surveys

A **questionnaire** is an on-screen or printed list of questions, and a **survey** is a research study that distributes a questionnaire to a large sample of participants. There are a number of means of distribution, including:

- post
- internet
- telephone
- handouts (for example, at the end of a class).

The questionnaire must be easy for the participants to understand without the researcher being present, in order for the data gathered to be accurate. Good design points include:

- avoiding leading questions
- avoiding jargon
- avoiding ambiguity
- avoiding emotive language.

> In either questionnaires or interviews, questions can be open (or 'open ended') or closed. An **open question** has a free choice of response. A **closed question** gives the participant a fixed selection of responses, such as yes/no, or numbers on a scale.

Evaluation of questionnaire surveys

Advantages
- Well-designed questionnaires with closed questions are relatively quick and easy to answer and can gather a lot of data.
- Answers can be analysed easily, forming totals and percentages.

Disadvantages
- Closed questions do not allow respondents to express opinions that are different from those offered. There may also be researcher bias in the selection of options.
- There is a risk of misunderstanding questions.
- There is a low response rate for postal questionnaires.

Interviews

The key characteristic of an **interview** is that questions are asked face-to-face, making research more time consuming, but allowing questions to be clarified where necessary.

There are three types of interview.

- An **unstructured interview** does not stick to a fixed list of questions, allowing the interviewer to vary their questioning depending on how a participant responds. Many open questions may be used, providing rich, detailed data.

- A **semi-structured interview** uses a set list of questions, but allows the interviewer some freedom. For example, the interviewer may ask the respondent to elaborate on some answers, or may switch the order of questions.

- A **structured interview** uses a fixed list of questions. It is therefore similar to a questionnaire survey, but conducted face-to-face. The interviewer will not go beyond the questions on the list, except to make clarifications.

Evaluation of interviews

Advantages

- Face-to-face format allows questions to be explained if necessary.

- Unstructured interviews can be personalised to each participant, and provide rich data.

Disadvantages

- Participants may distort the truth in order to look good to the interviewer. This is known as **social desirability bias.**

- Costly and time-consuming to run, and the data from open questions is harder to analyse.

> 🔍 **Top tip**
>
> Evaluation depends on the type of survey/interview and the type of questions used. Specify which type you mean in exam answers (for example, 'in an unstructured interview with open questions …').

Observation

An **observation** study involves watching behaviour as it happens. Data gathering involves an observer taking notes and (usually) categorising the behaviour they see – either at the time, or by later watching a recording.

Naturalistic

A **naturalistic observation** involves simply watching and recording whatever unfolds in a natural, everyday situation. It allows a researcher to gather data on spontaneous behaviour as it happens.

Participant

In a **participant observation**, one or more researchers takes part in the social situation. Participant observation gives the observer a unique insight into a social situation, and participants can more easily get used to their presence. However, it can lead to increased subjectivity, as the researcher becomes personally involved in the situation.

Disclosure

An observation can be **disclosed**, meaning that participants know they are being observed, or kept secret (**undisclosed**). Disclosing the observation has the problem that if people know they are being watched, this tends to change their behaviour. This is known as the **observer effect**. However, undisclosed observation may be unethical – it is never ethically acceptable to make secret observations of people in private, or to record them secretly. One way to minimise the observer effect is to give participants time to get used to the observer's presence.

Observation schedules

Some observation studies use a list of key behaviours called an **observation schedule**. This may require the observer to tick key behaviours each time they occur. By providing an objective standard, observation schedules can improve the reliability of recordings taken by more than one observer.

Inter-observer reliability means the extent to which two observers produce the same results when looking at the same data. This is never perfect, but well-trained observers usually show a high level of inter-observer reliability.

Evaluation of observation

Advantages

- Detailed record of real-life behaviour as it happens.
- Captures behaviour in its true social context.

Disadvantages

- Lacks the control of an experiment, so cannot infer cause-and-effect.
- Hard to replicate the results of an observational study, as each social situation is unique.

Case studies

A **case study** is another example of a non-experimental research method. It is an in-depth study, which is usually based on one individual case, but could also be conducted on a small group.

A case study is generally **longitudinal** – it follows participants over an extended period of time.

A case study will usually involve one or more of the other methods described earlier, such as interviews. Other techniques commonly used include ability tests, such as tests of IQ and memory, and brain scans.

Research examples

Case studies are done for various reasons, including the following.

- Many case studies have been conducted into the effects of brain damage on behaviour.
- In the area of sleep, case studies of extreme sleep deprivation have been carried out, and Freud used the method to build up his psychoanalytic theory of dreams.

Evaluation of case studies

Advantages

- Allows the researcher to focus on a specific instance and identify processes and variables.
- Insights from participant(s) may reveal an unusual and highly relevant perspective.

Disadvantages

- Results are specific to the individual, often impossible to replicate and it is hard to generalise findings to other people.
- Close relationship between researcher and participant(s) potentially interferes with objectivity.

Quick test

1. Which type of observation involves watching participants in their everyday environment?

2. Name one non-experimental research method that involves asking questions about people's thoughts and behaviour.

3. Briefly describe one strength and one weakness of the case study method.

4. Explain how an observation study is conducted. Consider some of the problems with this method of research, and how they might be overcome.

Key concepts

- Non-experimental methods
- Questionnaire
- Survey
- Open question
- Closed question
- Interview
- Structured interview
- Semi-structured interview
- Unstructured interview
- Social desirability bias
- Observation
- Naturalistic observation
- Observer effect
- Participant observation
- Disclosed/undisclosed
- Observation schedule
- Inter-observer reliability
- Case study
- Longitudinal

Data analysis and graphs

Qualitative vs. quantitative data

Some studies, for example interviews using open questions, produce **qualitative data**. These are non-numerical data such as descriptions. Most studies produce **quantitative data** – data based on numbers. This data can be analysed using statistics; and displayed in graphs.

Measures of central tendency

There are three main measures of central tendency – ways of showing the average or most typical value of a set of data: the mean, the mode and the median.

The mean

The **mean** is calculated by adding together all of the values and dividing by the number of scores. It includes all of the scores in the calculation, but can be distorted by extreme high or low scores.

The mode

The **mode** is the most common or popular score. This can be useful to avoid extreme values; however, some sets of data do not have a mode. If two or more numbers are equally the most common, the data are bimodal (two modes) or multimodal (several modes).

The median

The **median** is the midpoint of the data, obtained by putting scores in order, low to high, and finding the one in the centre. If there is an even number of scores, the mean of the middle two scores is calculated.

Measures of dispersion

Measures of central tendency alone give no indication of whether scores are generally close to or far away from the average. The purpose of measures of dispersion is to show how widely data are spread out.

The range

The **range** is the difference between the lowest and highest scores, calculated by subtracting the lowest from the highest. It is limited in that it doesn't reflect the distribution of the other data.

The standard deviation

The **standard deviation** shows the typical amount by which the scores in the distribution differ from the mean. The calculation is based on finding the difference between each score and the mean, and then calculating the average of these differences. An advantage is that all data are included in the calculation.

Graphs

Graphs are used to present results, and also to analysis. Commonly used types include the following.

- **Bar graph**: a bar graph shows scores as heights on two or more separated 'bars', which often represent the different conditions of an experiment. It allows for an easy comparison of means.

- **Pie chart**: a pie chart is not commonly used in psychology, but can be helpful for showing the percentages of a population that engage in a behaviour. The size of each slice represents its proportion; the total should add up to 100%. Scores on a DV such as memory test scores should not be presented on a pie chart.

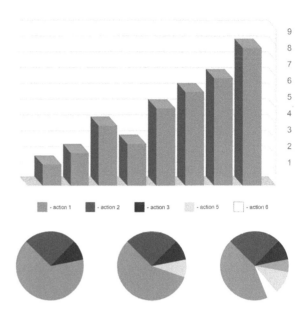

- action 1   - action 2   - action 3   - action 5   - action 6

Quick test

1. What type of graph would be suitable for displaying the findings of an experiment with three experimental conditions, and a DV based on percentage scores on a test?

2. A survey asks people about how long it takes them to get to sleep, and gets the following responses:

   30 mins   25 mins   10 mins   8 mins   60 mins

   What are the median and mean number of minutes taken to get to sleep among the sample?

🔑 Key concepts

- Qualitative data
- Quantitative data
- Mean
- Mode
- Median
- Range
- Standard deviation
- Bar graph
- Pie chart

Quick test answers

Chapter 1 Sleep and dreams

The biology of sleep

1. Circadian rhythms
2. Dreams
3. The hypothalamus
4. Adenosine

The restoration theory of sleep

1. Repairing injuries/removal of waste chemicals/replenishing neurotransmitters
2. A longer period of non-REM sleep.
3. They believed that REM sleep is essential for brain restoration, and slow-wave sleep is essential for bodily restoration.

Biological and psychoanalytic explanations of dreaming

1. Activation synthesis
2. It states that dreams have a hidden meaning relating to wish fulfilment.
3. Latent content

Cognitive processes in sleep and dreams

1. In order to make space and to avoid obsessions or hallucinations.
2. Neural network computer models of learning, in which reverse learning was shown to be useful.
3. No. Sleep is generally thought to be beneficial to memory, while a lack of sleep harms cognitive functioning.

Factors that affect sleep quality

1. The screen contains light and in particular a lot of blue wavelengths. These suppress melatonin release, affecting sleep.

2. Reduced alertness/depression/CHD/ digestive illnesses/etc.

Chapter 2 Depression

What is depression?

1. Such opinions are subjective, and highly influenced by social norms.
2. Every day for at least two weeks.

Biological explanations of depression

1. Serotonin
2. A predisposition in someone's biology or thought processes that makes them more vulnerable.

Biological treatments for depression

1. SSRIs and SNRIs
2. It modifies blood flow in the frontal lobe of the neocortex.

Cognitive explanations of depression

1. Self, world and future
2. CBT, or a combination of drugs and CBT

Chapter 3 Memory

The nature of memory

1. Episodic/semantic/procedural/visual LTM
2. Encoding, storage and retrieval

The multi-store model

1. Craik and Tulving (1975)

The working memory model

1. The central executive
2. The phonological loop (or the phonological store/articulatory process)

Forgetting

1 No, because information from working memory decays rapidly.

2 Proactive interference

3 Information may be difficult or impossible to retrieve from LTM without having actually decayed.

4 State cues, context cues and verbal cues

5 State cues: different amount of coffee/caffeine, and context cues: different time and location

6 c

Chapter 4 Stress

The physiology of stress

1 Running away (flight)

2 Animals were harmed in the research

Stress and health

1 Chronic stress

2 Depression and eating disorders (or panic disorder, schizophrenia, etc.)

3 Immunosuppression

Sources of stress

1 An environmental stressor

2 The social readjustment rating scale

3 It's less stressful to be at the top of the hierarchy, both in human organisations (Marmot et al) and primate groups (Sapolsky).

Individual differences in stress

1 In an internal locus of control – feeling that you are in control of what happens.

2 Commitment, control and challenge

Coping strategies

1 Benzodiazepines

2 Conceptualisation

3 The person may be taught skills/may practice skills/may use techniques such as role-playing and visualisation

4 Instrumental social support

Chapter 5 Conformity and obedience

The nature of conformity

1 Identification

2 Normative influence

3 Engineering students

Factors affecting conformity

1 The rise from two to three

2 False

3 They used both males and females as participants/their participants wore filter glasses that affected the length of line that they saw/there were no actors used/participants were acquaintances of one another/the group size was always four/it took place in Japan rather than in the USA.

4 Collectivist cultures

5 They used filter glasses that resulted in people seeing different lengths of lines.

Obedience

1 True

2 The agentic state

3 The authority figure being physically present

Chapter 6 Prejudice

Intergroup bias and discrimination

1 Examples could include rules that ban or restrict clothing or habits that are linked to a particular religion or that are more likely to target a particular ethnic group e.g. due to where they live or the languages they speak.

2 Groups based on race/sex/age/sexuality/disability etc.

3 The Equality Act of 2010

Explanations of prejudice

 1 A stereotype is one type of schema – an oversimplified or inaccurate mental category about a group of people.

2 The key idea is that we have stereotypes because the mind's resources are limited, so we take shortcuts.

3 Authoritarian submission

4 Right-wing authoritarianism

5 Previous comments made by research participants

Explanations of prejudice cont'd

1 Social categorisation/social identification/social comparison/psychological distinctiveness

2 Population validity – the difficulty in generalising the results to older ages or to other groups in society

Explanations of prejudice cont'd

1 Because they are competing for limited resources

2 Confirmation bias

Reducing prejudice

1 Eye colour

2 Superordinate goals

3 A specific education programme to tackle prejudice directly, particularly for people who have shown themselves to be bigots

4 No

5 A film, book or TV show could present characters that are authentic and real rather than stereotypes, for example by presenting a scientist who is a normal person rather than eccentric.

Chapter 7 Social relationships

Social exchange theory

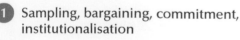 **1** Sampling, bargaining, commitment, institutionalisation

2 A way that people judge relationships, based on their schema/past relationships

Evolutionary theory

1 Both

2 Parental

Filter theory and investment theory

1 Availability (or category)

2 Equity and social network

Virtual relationships

1 Factors such as shyness that might make it harder for someone to initiate a face-to-face relationship.

2 False. People do share with strangers, and the internet may increase this.

3 Reduced cues theory

Parasocial relationships

1 The borderline pathological level

2 Insecure-resistant, because they are clingy and obsessive, and may prefer a relationship where they cannot be rejected.

3 The need for an ever greater 'fix' of information about the celebrity.

Chapter 8 Aggression

Biological influences on aggression

1 Instrumental aggression

2 In the limbic system

3 Foetal exposure to testosterone

Evolutionary and ethological explanations

1 In order to give people or animals an advantage in survival or reproduction

2 A behaviour from another member of our species that can prompt a fixed action pattern

Social learning theory

1 Observational (or 'vicarious') learning

2 Males

The use of music/the cat costume/the unrealistic background/labelling the video 'Herman the cat'

Theories of violence in institutions

 Convict sub-culture

 Situational attribution

Media influences on aggression

 Disinhibition

 Williams (1986) studied a region of Canada and found that the introduction of TV led to negative effects such as more aggressive behaviour, but a similar study by Charlton (1998) on the island of St Helena found no increases in aggression among the children there.

Chapter 9 Research

Ethical and scientific standards

 Equal

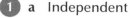 Volunteer sampling/self-selecting sampling

Experiments and variables

 a Independent

   b Dependent

 The null hypothesis

 a Specific vs. general practice

   b Skill at penalties; give them a test of penalty taking in the same conditions, such as with the same goalkeeper

   c Participants who engage in specific penalty practice will score more in a later test than participants who engage in general shooting practice.

   d Yes, to see whether either group improved compared to baseline.

 (Experimental) conditions

 By controlling extraneous variables and changing just one (the IV), the researcher can rule out any other cause of changes in the DV, and conclude that any changes must have been caused by the IV being manipulated.

Types of experiment

 Low/lack of ecological validity; this would be a problem because the behaviour studied might not generalise to the real world, making their results less useful and relevant.

 A quasi experiment: this would involve setting up an experimental task that prompts and measures aggression, such as a frustrating game to play. This could be done in a lab.

A natural experiment: this would study naturally occurring instances of aggression between the two groups, such as the frequency with which they get arrested for violent crime while shopping, or a self-report measure of aggression. This may have a confounding variable, as people in a shopping centre would be more likely to encounter provocation from strangers than would people shopping at home.

Non-experimental methods

 Naturalistic observation

 Interview OR survey

 Suitable answers could include: depth and volume of data; useful for unusual cases such as brain damage; longitudinal, so allows researcher to see changes; can be difficult to generalise to the rest of the population.

 Observation involves studying behaviour as it happens and recording data in the form of notes or videos. Includes naturalistic observation – observing a participant in an everyday context. Researcher may set out categories of behaviour in advance, with an observation schedule used to record these. Problems: a single observer can be unreliable; this problem can be overcome by training observers and also to use more than one. Inter-observer reliability means the extent to which different observers record the same data from the same observation. Ethical issues should be considered; invasion of privacy when people are observed without their consent. This must be avoided, though researchers should be aware that disclosing the observation will impact on the behaviour of participants. One way to minimise this problem is to ensure that participants being observed get used to the observer's presence

Data analysis and graphs

1 A bar graph

2 Median: 30 mins; mean: 26.6 mins

Part 2: Practice Question Book

1 Sleep and Dreams

Exercise 1A Multiple-choice questions

1 What is meant by the term 'circadian rhythms'? Choose one answer only.

a Different types of people who go to bed at different times.
b A group of brain areas that control sleep.
c Bodily processes that vary over a 24-hour cycle.
d A form of therapy for sleep disorders.

2 Which of the following is <u>not</u> true of melatonin? Choose one answer only.

a It is released into the bloodstream when it starts to get dark.
b It makes a person feel drowsy, and eventually fall asleep.
c It peaks in the middle of the night and then decreases towards daytime.
d Injections of it are offered to shift workers to help them stay alert.

3 Which of the following does <u>not</u> accurately describe a stage of sleep? Choose one answer only.

a Stage 1: in a light sleep.
b Stage 2: in a deep sleep, lasting 30 minutes.
c Stage 3: the EEG begins to show delta waves.
d Stage 4: groggy and disorientated if woken.

4 Which of the following was a feature of Dement & Kleitman's (1959) research study? Choose one answer only.

a It made use of a polysomnography.
b Participants were given sleeping pills.
c Participants were all female.
d Its main aim was to study shift work.

5 Which of the following best describes one of the variations in sleep patterns by age? Choose one answer only.

a Adults need at least nine hours of sleep per night.
b Newborns sleep less deeply than adults.
c Elderly people require more sleep than other ages.
d In adolescence, everybody becomes a 'night owl'.

6 Which of the following does <u>not</u> describe the brain's role in sleep? Choose one answer only.

a The brain cycles through sleep stages during the night.
b Sleep is important for the brain to consolidate memories.
c Caffeine builds up in our neurons during the night.
d The suprachiasmatic nucleus controls our body clock.

7 What is the term given to the part of the hypothalamus that plays a key role in the sleep-wake cycle? Choose one option only.

a The basal ganglia.

b The suprachiasmatic nucleus.

c The thalamus.

d The frontal lobe.

8 Which of the following is <u>not</u> a process restored during sleep, according to the restoration theory of sleep? Choose one option only.

a Repairing minor injuries.

b Deleting unwanted memories from the neocortex.

c Removal of waste chemicals in the muscles.

d Replenishing neurotransmitters in the brain.

9 Which of the following is the psychoanalytic term for the dream content that people can remember? Choose one answer only.

a Manifest.

b Preconscious.

c Latent.

d Repression.

10 Which of the following is <u>not</u> a feature of the reorganisational theory of sleep? Choose one answer only.

a The theory is based on computer models of memory.

b It stated that bad memories are deleted to avoid obsessions.

c It was devised by Crick and Mitchison in the 1980s.

d It states that REM sleep is needed to restore the brain.

Exercise 1B Biological processes in sleep

1 Complete the following sentence:

Sleep can be defined as a state of reduced conscious awareness during which the body is less active and less .... to the outside world.

2 During which stage of sleep do dreams mainly occur?

3 Complete the sentences by choosing the best words from the selection below. You do not have to use all the words:

> spindles   EEG   brain   fMRI   stages   REM   slow-wave

When we sleep, the brain goes through five sleep .... In stages 1–4, the body goes gradually into a deeper sleep, becoming harder to wake. The change from one stage to the next can be observed using the size and speed of electrical brain waves. Stages 3–4 feature large slow waves called delta waves, and these two stages in particular are sometimes called .... sleep. Psychologists study sleep stages using a recording of multiple changes in the brain and body called a polysomnography. An important part of this process is a brain monitor called an ....

4 Look at the example below. Briefly explain which sampling method is being used, and why might it have been chosen.

> Two researchers are recruiting participants for a lab experiment into sleep. They place adverts on a university noticeboard, announcing that the research involves an overnight stay in a sleep laboratory, and that participants must be over the age of 18 and in good health. Anyone who is interested is invited to email the researchers for further information.

5 Complete the following table:

Sleep stage	Feature
Stage 1	Easily woken
Stage 2	a
Stage 3	b
c	Groggy and disorientated if woken
d	Dreams occur

6 Which researchers conducted the 1957 study that established that REM sleep is dream sleep?

7 Look at the example below. Evaluate the methodology of the study.

> A team of researchers are conducting a study of sleep. They want to know what effect alcohol will have on dreams. They ask for volunteer participants, and five of their university colleagues agree to take part. Each volunteer is kept overnight in a sleep lab. Before sleep, they are given an alcoholic drink containing an amount of alcohol equivalent to two pints of lager. During the night, they are woken every half an hour and asked whether they were having a dream.

> **Hint** Consider the sample used, as well as the setting in which the research took place.

8 From the example above, identify two ethical issues that affect the study.

9 Briefly explain what is meant by the term 'circadian rhythms'.

10 Complete the sentences by choosing the best words from the selection below. You do not have to use all the words:

> repair   Freud   brain   hypothalamus   Oswald

The restoration theory of sleep states that the main function of sleep is that it is a period of down time that allows .... and maintenance, in much the same way that shutting down a factory could allow machines to be attended to. This theory, explained by .... (1966), states that all animals sleep because it allows the body and the .... to carry out these essential tasks.

11 Analyse the research evidence relating to the restoration theory of sleep.

> **Hint** Weigh up the research, considering whether it does or does not support the theory. Mention at least two studies.

Exercise 1C Explanations of dreaming

1 According to Freud, what is the basic psychological function of dreaming?

2 Complete the following table:

Term	Meaning
Latent content	a
Manifest content	b
Secondary elaboration	c

3 Explain the use of the case study method of research for sleep. Refer to the psychoanalytic approach to psychology.

4 Briefly explain one psychoanalytic defence mechanism that is relevant to the study of dreams.

5 Briefly explain one weakness of the psychoanalytic explanation of dreaming.

> Hint | Consider the research evidence.

6 How do biological psychologists explain the content of dreams?

7 Briefly explain the following key processes from the activation-synthesis theory:

a activation

b synthesis

8 Complete the sentences by choosing the best words from the selection below. You do not have to use all the words:

> distorting   information   perception   consolidating   brain   inventing

The cognitive approach to psychology explains behaviour in terms of beliefs and schemas. Cognitive psychologists think that the purpose of sleep and dreams is to facilitate .... processing, for example by .... memories.

9 Complete the following sentences about Crick and Mitchison's (1986) reorganisational theory of dreaming:

a Crick and Mitchison thought that the purpose of dreaming was to .... unwanted memories.

b There are two types of memories described in their theory: adaptive memories and .... memories.

c They thought that if the brain got cluttered with surplus information, this would lead to a person having .... or hallucinations.

d They used evidence from dolphins and .... to support their theory, as both of these animals have large brains and don't engage in REM sleep.

e A limitation of the theory is that modern neuroscience has shown that sleep .... memories rather than deleting them.

Exercise 1D Factors affecting sleep

1 Drinking caffeine and viewing light from a screen are two factors that can affect sleep. Explain why the time of day someone drinks caffeine OR views a screen could affect whether it harms their sleep quality. Refer to research.

2 Briefly explain two reasons that Niamh might be staying up late rather than going to sleep.

> Niamh is a 16-year-old girl who likes to stay up late. She regularly stays up later than everyone else in her family, and feels very tired the next morning.

3 Answer the following questions about the research by Czeisler et al. (1990), 'Exposure to bright light and darkness to treat physiologic maladaptation to night work':

a What was the IV in the study?

b Who were the participants in the study?

c What tasks were participants asked to do while they were in the lab?

d For how many days did the study last?

e What was the main conclusion of the study.

> **Make the link**
>
> See page 37 for a description of the Czeisler et al. research.

4 Place the stages in the correct order in the following diagram, to show how light affects sleep:

A: The suprachiasmatic nucleus reacts to light.

↓

B: The retina perceives light or darkness from the outside world.

↓

C: The retina sends a message to the brain.

↓

D: Melatonin is released into the bloodstream and causes drowsiness.

↓

E: The hypothalamus directs the pineal gland to release melatonin.

5 Draw a simple sketch or graph indicating how the brain cycles through different sleep stages across a whole night's sleep.

Exercise 1E Extended scenario

Look at the following example of individual behaviour, and answer the questions that follow:

> Kaiynat is a 19-year-old student who is finding it hard to get to sleep at night. On Friday and Saturday nights, Kaiynat works evening shifts in a restaurant. She gets home at 2 a.m. or later, and tends to stay up watching videos for another hour or two before going to bed. She also gets up very late on Saturday and Sundays.
>
> On week nights Kaiynat goes to bed much earlier, but tends to lie awake for at least an hour before dropping off. Sometimes she gets up and has a cup of coffee or a snack, or scrolls through messages on her phone. At times, she finds that messages from her social media contacts are playing on her mind when she's lying in bed. At other times she can't sleep because she feels stressed about deadlines for her studies.

1. Identify two lifestyle factors that could be affecting Kaiynat's sleep.

2. Analyse the role of circadian rhythms in Kaiynat's sleep problems.

3. What biological factors influence whether Kaiynat falls asleep or not?

4. Describe how Kaiynat could improve her sleep habits. Refer to research evidence in your answer.

Exercise 1F Integrating research understanding

Look at the following research study into individual behaviour, and answer the questions that follow.

Two student researchers are conducting a study into the effects of caffeine on alertness. In one condition, participants will be given a fairly high level of caffeine, and in another condition they will be given zero caffeine. They decide to measure alertness by giving participants a computerised test of their reaction time.

To control for extraneous variables and demand characteristics, the researchers decide to give the caffeine in the form of a mug of strong filter coffee, and to give the control condition a mug of decaffeinated coffee without telling participants which they are getting.

They gather their sample by approaching a nearby revision class, and – with the teacher's permission – asking the students if they are willing to come out of class for a few minutes to take part in a brief psychological test. They also inform participants that the second condition of the experiment will take place a week later.

Testing is done in an empty classroom that the researchers have set up as a lab for the study. On the first day of testing, each participant is given a cup of coffee, either caffeinated or decaf. Five minutes later, they are given the reaction time test. The following week they are given the other type of coffee, and then five minutes later do a different version of the reaction time test. Half of the participants drank caffeinated coffee in week one, and the other half drank decaf in week one. Which of these conditions they did first was decided by tossing a coin.

Participants are debriefed after the second condition.

1. What research method was used in the example above?

2. Briefly explain two examples of good ethical practice from the study above, with reference to the BPS researcher code of ethics.

3. Briefly explain two ethical problems in the study above.

4. Why did the researchers toss a coin when deciding which condition participants would do first? Are there any problems with this technique?

5. Why didn't researchers give everyone the same type of coffee in weeks 1 and 2 of the study?

6. Why did the researchers not inform participants what type of coffee they were getting?

7. Briefly explain what effects the research might have on the participants' sleep later the same day?

8. Briefly explain what effects the research might have on the participants' sleep the following day?

2 Depression

Exercise 2A Multiple-choice questions

1 Which of the following is <u>not</u> a diagnostic symptom of depression? Choose one answer only.

   a Low energy or feeling agitated.

   b Lack of enjoyment in one's usual activities.

   c Irrational fears of social situations.

   d Difficulty in concentrating.

2 Which of the following is <u>not</u> a feature of the DSM-5? Choose one answer only.

   a It is used to diagnose people with disorders such as depression and phobias.

   b It lists 271 different psychological disorders, categorised into groups.

   c The letters stand for 'disorder and symptom manual'.

   d Diagnosis is based on how many symptoms people show, and for how long.

3 Which of the following is <u>not</u> a mood disorder? Choose one answer only.

   a Major depression

   b PDD

   c Phobia

   d Bipolar disorder

4 Which of the following is thought to be true about the biology of depression? Choose one answer only.

   a Depression is linked to a more effective sleep-wake cycle.

   b Depression can be caused by hormones.

   c Certain people's brains lack a hypothalamus, causing depression.

   d Depression is largely caused by having a depressed twin.

5 Identify an evaluation point relating to the monoamine hypothesis of depression. Choose one answer only.

   a The hypothesis doesn't state which neurotransmitters are involved.

   b It focuses entirely on hormones.

   c Everybody gets depressed at some point, so the theory is inaccurate.

   d It fails to take account of social processes.

6 What causes depression, according to the diathesis–stress model? Choose one answer only.

   a Life events and a predisposition.

   b Genes and distorted beliefs.

   c Hormones and serotonin.

   d Sleep and electro-convulsive therapy.

7 Which of the following is true of a CBT therapy session? Choose one answer only.

    a The patient generally lies on a couch.
    b The therapist avoids being directive.
    c The therapist interprets the patient's dreams.
    d The session is like a structured meeting.

8 Which of the following is a reason that CBT might be preferred to chemotherapy for depression in some cases? Choose one answer only.

    a CBT is very quick.
    b CBT doesn't have major adverse side effects.
    c There are multiple types of CBT that can be tried.
    d CBT doesn't involve going to hospital.

9 Which type of antidepressant tackles serotonin and norepinephrine? Choose one answer only.

    a SSRIs
    b SNRIs
    c Tricyclics
    d MAOIs

10 Which of the following is a side-effect of ECT? Choose one answer only.

    a Sleep disturbances
    b Memory loss
    c Nausea
    d Suicidal thoughts

Exercise 2B Types of depression

1 Besides a severely unhappy mood, what is the key symptom of depression?

2 Briefly describe DSM-5.

3 Copy and fill in the following table:

Definition of abnormality based on …	Objective or subjective?	Example question that a psychologist could ask
Frequency/severity	a	How many people experience this behaviour?
Social norms	Subjective	b
c	Objective	Is the patient able to maintain healthy relationships?

4 Explain what is meant by major depressive disorder.

> **Hint** Ensure that you mention the two key diagnostic symptoms, and give examples of other typical symptoms. Describe the timescale of a diagnosis, and how frequent the disorder is.

5 Complete the sentences by choosing the best words from the selection below. You do not have to use all the words.

> anxiety dysthymia symptoms episodes severity five two

Another diagnosis described in DSM-5 is persistent depressive disorder (PDD), also known as .... The key difference between PDD and major depression is its duration and .... Major depression is characterised by shorter, more severe episodes, while PDD is long-lasting and less severe. In diagnostic terms, a patient could be diagnosed with PDD even if they show fewer .... than would be required for a diagnosis of major depression, but must show them for .... years or more.

6 Note down whether each of the following concepts link to neurochemistry, hormones, or the role of diathesis–stress.

  a Serotonin

  b Higher than average vulnerability

  c The thyroid

  d A twin study

  e The monoamine hypothesis

7 Summarise the McGuffin et al. (1996) twin study of depression, or another study into the biology of depression. Put one key point beside each heading:

  • Aim:

  • Methodology:

  • Findings/results:

  • Conclusion:

  • A strength of the study:

  • A weakness of the study:

> **Make the link**
>
> See page 43 for a description of the McGuffin research.

8 **a** Briefly explain 'diathesis' in the diathesis–stress model, and give an example.

  b Briefly explain 'stress' in the diathesis–stress model, and give an example.

9 Briefly evaluate biological explanations of depression.

> **Hint** When evaluating these explanations in general, try to think of what the different explanations have in common.

Exercise 2C Treatments for depression

 1 True or false – side effects from SSRIs tend to improve within a few weeks. Briefly explain your choice.

2 Look at the following example of individual behaviour:

> For a long while, Zander has been experiencing unhappiness and stress. He finds it hard to sleep soundly, and his mood is low and depressed. He used to play guitar every day when he was younger, but these days he can't be bothered.

a Briefly explain what disorder Zander may have.

b Explain what further information a doctor or psychologist would need to know about Zander's case.

c Briefly explain what biological treatment might be used to help Zander.

3 Explain the use of electroconvulsive therapy, referring to research evidence.

> Hint Explain what ECT is, as well as its effects and any relevant evidence about how effective it is.

4 Complete the following sentences:

a By reducing brain cells' ability to re-uptake (i.e. reabsorb) .... , SSRIs cause more of this neurotransmitter to be available in the brain.

b SNRIs are slightly less specific in their action than SSRIs, as they tackle not just serotonin but also ...., another monoamine neurotransmitter.

c The more common side effects of tricyclics include .... vision, constipation, memory impairments and increased body temperature.

d Monoamine oxidase inhibitors (MAOIs) are an older type of antidepressant drug, now most often used for .... disorders or bipolar mood disorder.

5 Decide whether each of the following statements is true or false.

Statement	True	False
SSRI antidepressants are considered safe to use with children and adolescents by the Food and Drug Administration (FDA) in the USA		
ECT is used to treat depression if an SSRI drug doesn't help a patient straight away.		
A newer generation of MAOIs, known as 'reversible inhibitors of monoamine oxidase A' (RIMAs), has been developed, but they are more widely used for social phobias than for depression.		

Exercise 2D Cognitive approach to depression

1 Briefly explain what is meant by a negative self-schema.

2 a Briefly explain Beck's cognitive triad.

b Give one example of each of the three aspects of the triad.

c Briefly explain how these beliefs develop.

d How easy is it to change a person's cognitive triad?

3 Place the stages in the correct order in the following diagram, to show Ellis's explanation of how life events can trigger depression: belief / event / consequence

A)

B)

C)

4 Explain what Ellis meant by 'faulty information processing'.

5 Look at the following example of individual behaviour:

> Akash is worried about a question that he got wrong in his Higher History prelim. He made a silly mistake, and now thinks that this means that his knowledge isn't good enough. This has frequently been keeping him awake at night. It's now May, and Akash has been working hard in preparation for his final exam. His parents tell him he should take a break, but he says he can't – he doesn't want to make another mistake.

Explain how the cognitive theory of depression would interpret Akash's situation.

6 Briefly explain what is meant by cognitive restructuring.

7 Analyse the use of cognitive behavioural therapy for depression, referring to evidence.

> 🔍 **Top tip**
>
> Evidence on the use of CBT can be used when explaining cognitive theories of depression, or when asked to explain/analyse research into treatments for depression.

Exercise 2E Extended scenario

Briefly look at the following example of individual behaviour, and answer the questions that follow:

Günther is an office worker who is also a successful basketball player. In his spare time, he likes jogging and listening to music. However, recently he has been finding it hard to get motivated. He is finding the music that he previously enjoyed boring and repetitive, and he finds it very hard to get up in the morning and go running or go to basketball training. In fact, he has missed most of his training sessions for the past few weeks, and has been dropped from the team. He has also not been eating much except junk food. Overall, Günther is feeling low and depressed.

Günther's flatmate is worried about him, and suggests that he sees a doctor. Günther agrees, and his doctor asks if anything triggered his recent feelings. Günther explains that a couple of months ago, he broke up with his partner, with whom he had previously been in a relationship for five years. Since then, he explains, he has felt like a worthless human being, and that there is no point in trying to improve his situation.

1. What symptoms does Günther have that could suggest a diagnosis of major depressive disorder? List all that apply.

2. What biological factors influence whether someone becomes depressed?

3. Explain Günther's case in terms of the diathesis–stress model of depression.

4. What kind of treatments might the doctor recommend to Günther, and are they effective? Refer to research evidence in your answer.

Exercise 2F Integrating research understanding

1. Interviews and surveys are often used to ask people about their mood. Evaluate the use of the interview method with research participants.

Look at the following research study into individual behaviour, and answer the questions that follow.

An international team of researchers is investigating the role of beliefs in persistent depressive disorder. They want to know what people with the disorder believe about themselves, the world and the future, and whether these beliefs are linked to the severity of their symptoms.

They decide to gather data using closed questions. They recruit participants via an email to local university students, asking anyone who has been diagnosed with any form of depression to click a link, which takes them to an online questionnaire. This questionnaire has a consent form at the start. It asks participants about their diagnosis and symptoms, as well as about their beliefs. At the end, participants are identified by a unique code, which they can use if they wish to later withdraw their data from the study.

The study shows participants' responses to questions about their beliefs, which the researchers calculate as percentages. These show that most people with the symptoms of persistent depressive disorder have very negative views about the world and the future, while their beliefs about themselves are more positive. Nearly everyone questioned shows some form of inaccurate or distorted belief. The researchers conclude that beliefs play a role in the prognosis of the disorder.

A small number of participants are approached via email and asked to take part in follow-up research, which will be longitudinal.

2 What are the symptoms of persistent depressive disorder?

3 What research method was used in the example above?

4 What sampling technique was used in the study above?

5 Briefly explain what is meant by:

   a open questions

   b closed questions

6 Briefly explain two ways in which the researchers in the study above followed an ethical code.

7 What term is used by psychologists to describe negative beliefs about the self, the world and the future?

8 Explain why the researchers thought that beliefs would play a role in persistent depressive disorder.

9 Explain why the researchers wanted to follow up the questionnaire study with a longitudinal study.

3   Memory

Exercise 3A Multiple-choice questions

1 Which of the following is a memory store with a very brief duration? Choose one answer only.

   a Cue-dependent memory

   b Episodic memory

   c Long-term memory

   d Sensory memory

2 Which of the following refers to the memory process where information is brought back to mind when needed? Choose one answer only.

   a Retrieval

   b Attention

   c Storage

   d Rehearsal

3 Which of the following is <u>not</u> one of the stores of the multi-store model? Choose one answer only.

   a Sensory memory

   b Long-term memory

   c Semantic memory

   d Working memory

4 What term is used to describe superior recall of the first few items from a list? Choose one answer only.

   a The primacy effect

   b The serial position curve

   c The spacing effect

   d Episodic memory

5 Which of the following was <u>not</u> a feature of the Murdock (1962) experiment? Choose one answer only.

   a Participants were given lists of random words to remember.

   b Words at the start of the list were better remembered.

   c It provided evidence for two separate memory stores.

   d It showed researchers which brain areas are involved in memory.

6 Which of the following is <u>not</u> a part of the working memory model (Baddeley, 2000)? Choose one answer only.

   a The phonological loop

   b The short-term store

   c The central executive

   d The episodic buffer

7 Which of the following is true of the information that you study or learn about during your classes? Choose one answer only.

a   All of it enters LTM, but only for 1–2 seconds.

b   It is permanently stored in the frontal lobe of the brain.

c   It only includes procedural memories for skills.

d   These memories become harder to retrieve over time.

8 Which of the following can act as a cue, making forgetting less likely? Choose one answer only.

a   A meaningless trigram

b   The appearance of a room

c   The hippocampus

d   An entirely new piece of information

9 Which of the following is true of a person's childhood memories? Choose one answer only.

a   They are highly resilient, even if you suffer brain damage.

b   They are stored in your working memory.

c   They are mainly sensory memories.

d   They only include procedural memories for skills.

10 Which of the following refers to forgetting where memories are lost or become inaccessible solely due to the passage of time? Choose one answer only.

a   Proactive interference

b   Retroactive interference

c   Trace decay

d   Cue dependent forgetting

Exercise 3B Memory stores

1 Which memory store briefly stores sensations, allowing things that we see and hear to be retained long enough for us to focus our attention on them?

2 What brain areas are particularly crucial for the healthy functioning of:

a   working memory

b   LTM

3 Copy and fill in the following table:

Type of LTM	Definition	Example of use
Episodic	a	Remembering something you did yesterday.
b	Memory for physical skills.	Learning how to throw a basketball.
c	Memory for word meanings and facts.	d

4 Explain how working memory and LTM are used in the real world, giving examples.

5 Complete the sentences by choosing the best words from the selection below. You do not have to use all the words.

> removed   encoding   storage   distortion   rehearsal   retrieved

Regardless of which type of memory is being studied, a logical set of processes must take place. First, information must enter the memory store. This is known as .... Then it must remain there for a period of time until it is needed or until it can be moved to another store. This process is known as .... Finally, it must be .... from the store and used or moved to another store.

6 Note down whether each of the following examples relate to the memory processes of encoding, storage or retrieval.

a Reading a news story.

b Telling somebody a joke that you heard last week.

c A person keeping the names of a few food items in mind as they walk to the shops.

d Someone seeing a place and realising that they had been there before.

7 Complete the sentences by choosing the best words from the selection below. You do not have to use all the words.

> contrasted   personality   expectations   problems   emotions   linked

Long-term memories are interconnected sets of knowledge schemas. New learning isn't stored separately (as might happen with a computer) but is interpreted and .... to existing knowledge. As Bartlett showed, memories can be distorted to make them more like our cultural ...., subtracting elements that don't fit. These interconnected long-term memories can even play a role in solving ...., demonstrating that they do not sit inertly in storage until we choose to retrieve them (Ericsson & Kintsch, 1995).

Exercise 3C The multi-store model

1 According to the multi-store model, what process is necessary for items to be transferred from working memory (the short-term store) to LTM?

2 Do people learn new skills through storing information in sensory memory?

3 Briefly explain how sensory memory is used in everyday life.

4 Which of the following graphs shows the serial position curve?

A)

B)

C)

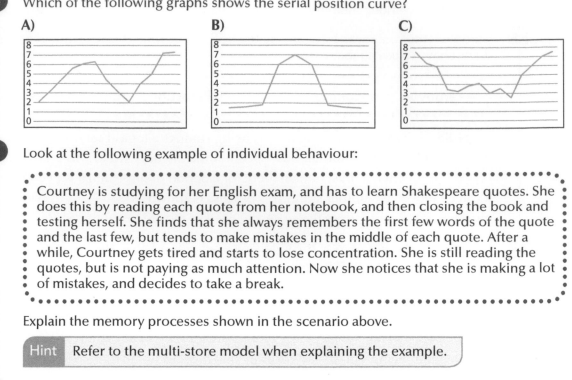

5 Look at the following example of individual behaviour:

Courtney is studying for her English exam, and has to learn Shakespeare quotes. She does this by reading each quote from her notebook, and then closing the book and testing herself. She finds that she always remembers the first few words of the quote and the last few, but tends to make mistakes in the middle of each quote. After a while, Courtney gets tired and starts to lose concentration. She is still reading the quotes, but is not paying as much attention. Now she notices that she is making a lot of mistakes, and decides to take a break.

Explain the memory processes shown in the scenario above.

> **Hint** Refer to the multi-store model when explaining the example.

6 Evaluate the multi-store model, using research evidence.

Exercise 3D The working memory model

1 Which part(s) of the working memory model would be involved if a person was asked to count to twenty?

2 Complete the following sentences:

a Baddeley and Hitch believed that working memory is a flexible, active store with which we carry out numerous .... tasks such as holding a conversation, playing a game or following a map.

b A central ...., based on attention, controls other parts of the model, which are known as slave systems.

c The phonological loop processes .... information inside your head.

d The visuo-spatial .... does routine visual processing.

3 Explain the <u>findings</u> of the word length effect study by Baddeley, Thomson and Buchanan (1975), or another study relating to the working memory model. Put one key point beside each heading:

> **Make the link**
>
> See page 55 for a description of the Baddeley et al. research.

- Aim:
- Methodology:
- Findings/results:
- Conclusion:
- A strength of the study:
- A weakness of the study:

Exercise 3E Forgetting

1 True or false – forgetting occurs in all memory stores for the same reasons. Briefly explain your answer.

2 Which type of interference is involved if you can remember your new address, but have forgotten your old one?

3 Complete the sentences by choosing the best words from the selection below. You do not have to use all the words.

> seconds   minutes   hours   working   episodic   maintenance

Decay theory applies particularly to sensory and .... memory, and follows from the idea that these stores have a very limited duration. Sensory memory is thought to be limited to a couple of .... at most. WM duration is also very brief if the person does not make use of .... rehearsal. Decay fits with people's everyday assumptions and experience – it is easy for something to quickly leave our minds, such as when a person tells you their name and you find that a couple of .... later you can't recall it.

4 Explain a task and suitable materials that could be used for an experiment on decay.

> **Hint** You can base your answer around a real study that you have read about.

5 Briefly explain two different ideas about how decay affects LTM.

6 Do students predict that information they study will decay?

7 Look at the following example of individual behaviour:

> Jamie has lost his house keys, and is trying to remember where he last saw them. First, he checks in his car, but they aren't there. Then he realises that he put the keys in the glove box of his car yesterday, but has since moved them. He recalls putting something into his pocket recently, but when he checks, all that is there is his phone.

Explain the scenario in terms of interference explanations of forgetting.

8 Decide whether each of the following statements is true or false.

Statement	True	False
Memories are always forgotten eventually.		
It is hard to remember old memories out of context.		
Memories can be triggered by a cue.		
A person's entire LTM can be destroyed by damage to a single small area of the brain.		

9 Cues can affect memory and forgetting. Briefly describe two types of cue, with examples.

10 On the basis of the psychological research into context cues, should you do all of your revision in the school/college library?

11 Look at the following example of individual behaviour:

> Dimitrios, age 10, went on holiday with his parents last summer. When he returned to school, he tried to write a description of what he did on holiday, but found some details hard to recall. Later that day he discussed the holiday with his older sister, and found that she remembered the events quite differently from what he had written in class.

Discuss why Dimitrios and his sister have different memories of their shared holiday.

Make the link

See page 58 for a description of the study of H.M.

12 Explain what effects H.M.'s brain damage had on his memory.

Exercise 3F Extended scenario

Look at the following example of individual behaviour, and answer the questions that follow:

> Karel is a science student at college. He is working through a course that will prepare him to apply for a degree in Medicine next year. It's an important year, and he spends a couple of hours every evening studying and revising.
>
> During his study sessions, Karel tends to listen to music. However, he finds that the lyrics of the music can be distracting, and at times he accidentally writes down a word from one of the songs instead of a science term in his notes.
>
> Karel has been making use of diagrams such as mind maps and concept maps. These show the different terms in his topics connected together with others that have related meanings, such as the different glands in the body.
>
> A friend who studies psychology has advised Karel to test himself frequently, and to space out his study by dividing his study of a particular topic over several days, rather than doing it all in the one evening. Karel finds it hard to remember new terminology, and his friend advises him to rehearse these multiple times, saying them to himself while doing something else.

1 Briefly explain how Karel's learning involves the processes of encoding, storage and retrieval.

2 Explain the above scenario with reference to Baddeley's working memory model.

3 Explain how forgetting may play a role in Karel's learning process.

4 Evaluate the study advice that Karel received. Refer to research evidence in your answer.

Exercise 3G Integrating research understanding

1 Interviews and surveys are often used to ask people with memory problems about their experience. Evaluate the use of the interview method with this type of research participants.

Look at the following research study into individual behaviour, and answer the questions that follow.

> An international team of researchers is investigating the role of brain damage in forgetting. They believe that excessive use of alcohol is likely to damage brain cells, leading to more forgetting than more moderate alcohol use.
>
> They decide to gather data using questionnaires. They recruit participants via an email to local university students, asking anyone who regularly consumes alcohol to click a link, which takes them to an online questionnaire. The questionnaire features a set of closed questions, and has a consent form at the start. It asks participants about the amount and frequency of their alcohol use, as well as about situations where they have forgotten appointments or other important information. At the end, participants are given a unique code that they can use if they wish to later withdraw their data from the study.
>
> The study shows participants' experiences and behaviour, which the researchers calculate as percentages. This shows that people who tend to drink a lot of alcohol in a single day also experience a lot of forgetting, compared to those who consume the drug over longer timescales. The researchers conclude that exposure to high levels of alcohol is toxic to brain cells, and that this affects memory.
>
> A small number of participants are approached via email and asked to take part in follow-up research, which will be longitudinal.

2 What brain areas are involved in memory?

3 What research method was used in the example above?

4 What sampling technique was used in the study above?

5 Briefly explain what is meant by:

  a open questions

  b closed questions

6 Briefly explain two ways in which the researchers in the study above followed an ethical code.

7 What three terms mean long-term memory for physical skills, life events and factual information?

8 Explain why the researchers thought that alcohol use might lead to forgetting.

9 Explain why the researchers wanted to follow up the questionnaire study with a longitudinal study.

4 Stress

Exercise 4A Multiple-choice questions

1 Which of the following describes the body's response to acute stress? Choose one option only.

   a Fight-or-flight

   b Shame-or-refrain

   c Rest-or-digest

   d Selye-or-hellyeah

2 Which of the following is an example of chronic stress? Choose one option only.

   a A person has had a bad day at work.

   b A pupil is stressed throughout S5.

   c A couple are stressed by having an argument.

   d A man is stressed because he missed a bus.

3 Which of the following is <u>not</u> one of the stages of the general adaptation syndrome? Choose one option only.

   a Alarm

   b Resistance

   c Adaptation

   d Exhaustion

4 Which of the following can be an indirect effect of long-term stress?

   a Raised blood pressure

   b Coronary heart disease

   c Improved memory

   d Increased smoking and drinking

5 Which of the following <u>reduces</u> when you experience long-term stress? Choose one option only.

   a Moodiness/grumpiness

   b The number of white blood cells in your bloodstream.

   c The level of cortisol in your saliva.

   d The frequency with which you get colds.

6 Which of the following is a characteristic of Type-A behaviour? Choose one option only.

   a Worried

   b Cooperative

   c Hostile

   d Relaxed

7 Which of the following is <u>not</u> one of the '3 Cs' of hardiness?

    a Commitment

    b Clarity

    c Challenge

    d Control

8 Which of the following is <u>not</u> involved in the hypothalamic–pituitary–adrenal system? Choose one option only.

    a The pituitary gland

    b ACTH

    c The adrenal medulla

    d Cortisol

9 Which of the following is <u>not</u> a major cause of occupational stress? Choose one option only.

    a Workload

    b Lack of control

    c Noise

    d Immunosuppression

10 Which of the following is a drug therapy for stress? Choose one option only.

    a Melatonin

    b Beta blockers

    c Amphetamine

    d Chocolate

Exercise 4B The physiology of stress

1 True or false – stress is our reaction to demands that exceed our ability to cope.

2 What is meant by 'acute stress'?

3 Decide whether each of the following are changes that occur during fight or flight:

Change	True or False
Heart rate rises	
Muscles become more tense	
The person becomes weaker	
Glucose is released	
Breathing becomes faster	
Digestion gets faster	

4 Complete the sentences by choosing the best words from the selection below. You do not have to use all the words.

> physiology   die   dangers   energy   gene   stone-age   sweat

When faced by an immediate severe threat, an organism's body prepares to fight, or to run away ('flight'). In this acute stress response, the body gets ready to expend .... and use its muscles. The first humans lived a hunter-gatherer existence, where fight-or-flight helped them to survive from immediate .... However, in the modern world this response to stress is often unhelpful. For example, the fight-or-flight response may cause a person to .... when giving a speech. Such threats have not been around for long enough to make a significant difference to the human .... pool.

5 Which stage of the general adaptation syndrome includes the changes seen in the acute stress response?

6 What are diseases of adaptation?

7 Summarise Selye's (1936) study of rats, or another study into the physiology of stress. Put one key point beside each heading:

- Aim:
- Methodology:
- Findings/results:
- Conclusion:
- A strength of the study:
- A weakness of the study:

> **☀ Make the link**
>
> See page 62 for a description of Selye's research.

8 Explain the health effects of acute stress.

> Hint   Think of examples of brief or temporary health problems, rather than long-term illnesses.

9 What type of locus of control is associated with higher stress?

10 **a** Explain two key differences between the physiological system that triggers a stress response via the sympathetic nervous system, and the system that triggers a stress response via the hypothalamus.

b Explain how these two systems help the body to release energy to tackle stress.

11 Look at the following example of individual behaviour:

> Freya is travelling to a concert – she has tickets for herself and two friends. Her usual train into town has been cancelled, so she decides to go by taxi. However, major roadworks cause a delay, and she arrives half an hour late. She meets with her friends, who are very annoyed that they have missed the start of the show. Freya feels very tense in her muscles, and the following day wakes up with a sore throat.

Explain Freya's situation in terms of stress and immunosuppression.

12 Decide whether each of the following statements is true or false:

Statement	True or False
Some of the health effects of stress are side effects of processes that occur for other reasons.	
Long-term stress can worsen skin conditions.	
Both adrenaline and cortisol function to increase the glucose (blood sugar) level in the bloodstream.	
Raised levels of glucose in the bloodstream don't carry any risk to health.	

13 Complete the sentences by choosing the best words from the selection below. You do not have to use all the words.

blocking   leucocytes   immune   GAS   healed   suppression

The .... system is essential for healing infected areas of the body and for fighting off viruses. A key part of the immune system is the lymph (or lymphatic) system, a set of body areas that produce white blood cells called .... The body can cope with brief periods of stress, but if stress is prolonged, the production of leucocytes is reduced, making the body more vulnerable to infection and slower to heal. In one study, researchers found that an injury .... faster among the control group than among people who were chronically stressed. However, exercise can modify the harmful effects of stress, and can reduce the .... of leucocytes.

Exercise 4C Sources of stress and individual differences

1 True or false – humans are social animals, and therefore do not get stressed by social situations.

2 Copy and fill in the following table:

Type of stressor	Example	One example research finding
Occupational		
Environmental		
Social		

3 a Briefly describe the SRRS scale and explain how it is used.
   b Give two example items from the SRRS scale.
   c Explain one weakness of using questionnaires to study people's stressors.

4 Briefly discuss what role control can have on occupational or workplace stress.

5 Identify one personality trait, and briefly state how it might affect stress.

6 Briefly explain what is meant by 'hardiness', in the context of stress.

7 Briefly explain one type of individual difference that can affect stress, other than personality and hardiness.

8 Explain how individual differences can affect stress, with reference to one study such as Friedman and Rosenman's (1974) study of type A and type B behaviour.

> **Make the link**
>
> See page 69 for a description of Friedman and Rosenman's research.

Exercise 4D Coping strategies for stress

1 Complete the following sentence:

Drug therapy can be used to directly tackle the stress .... in the body. Such drugs are frequently prescribed by GPs for stress-related problems.

2 Briefly describe some of the main side effects associated with benzodiazepines and beta blockers.

3 Match the stages of stress inoculation therapy to the descriptions:

Conceptualisation Phase	Coping skills are taught and practiced with the therapist.
Skills Acquisition Phase	Clients are taught to break stressors down into smaller units, in order to tackle them.
Application Phase	Newly acquired skills are used in real-life stressful situations.

4 Give a strength and a weakness of the use of stress inoculation therapy or CBT to treat stress.

5 The Nuckolls et al. (1972) research into social support and stress was a natural experiment. Analyse the use of natural experiments to study stress. Make at least three points.

Exercise 4E Extended scenario

Look at the following example of individual behaviour, and answer the questions that follow:

Lorenzo is a researcher who has recently moved to Scotland to work for a private research firm. This company conducts research into the environment, and applies for government funding to develop responses to climate change. Lorenzo works in a rather cramped room, with a desk, lots of piles of papers, and no window.

Over the past few weeks, one of Lorenzo's colleagues has been off sick, and Lorenzo has therefore taken on extra work. He is finding it very hard to get through his daily tasks, and often takes work home to complete it late in the evening. He finds this difficult, in part because he has very noisy neighbours. He has asked them to stop playing loud music when he's trying to work, but it hasn't stopped them doing so.

When he's at work, Lorenzo is frequently interrupted by his manager who tells him to stop what he's doing and work on something else instead. As a result, he feels that he has little control over what he does and when he does it. He feels that if he could just get to grips with his backlog of tasks for a few days he could make real progress, but every time this task list gets shorter, he is given more things to do. The manager is aggressive and always in a rush; she also frequently reminds him that his work needs to be finished quickly or the whole office could lose out on an important contract.

When he's feeling particularly stressed, Lorenzo calls his sister and has a long chat by phone. She isn't able to be of any practical help, but these conversations make him feel a lot better about things.

1 Briefly explain <u>four</u> sources of stress that Lorenzo is experiencing.

2 Explain Lorenzo's experiences with reference to the concepts of control and workload.

3 Explain the concept of hardiness OR type A behaviour with reference to the scenario above.

> Hint | Make links between traits associated with your chosen concept and Lorenzo or another character in the scenario.

4 What type of social support is Lorenzo getting? Explain its effects.

Exercise 4F Integrating research understanding

1 Interviews and surveys are often used to ask people about stress that they experience in the workplace or their relationships. Evaluate the use of the interview method to investigate social/occupational stress.

Look at the following research study into individual behaviour, and answer the questions that follow.

An international team of researchers is investigating immunosuppression. They want to find out what social, environmental and occupational stressors people have experienced over the past six months, and also to find out about each person's level of health.

They decide to gather data using questionnaires. They recruit participants via an email to local construction workers. The questionnaire features a set of closed questions, and has a consent form at the start. It asks participants about day-to-day hassles that they have experienced, as well as about health problems such as headaches, mouth ulcers or colds. At the end, participants are given a unique code that they can use if they wish to later withdraw their data from the study.

The study shows participants' responses to each type of health issue and stressor, and the researchers calculate these as percentages. The findings show that participants have experienced a higher rate of health problems following social stress compared to occupational and environmental stressors. The researchers conclude that social stressors impact on us more because it is harder to control these sort of stressors, and they tend to be more prolonged.

A small number of participants are approached via email and asked to take part in follow-up research, which will be longitudinal.

2 Explain what is meant by immunosuppression.

3 What research method was used in the example above?

4 What sampling technique was used in the study above?

5 Briefly explain what is meant by:
a open questions
b closed questions

6 Briefly explain two ways in which the researchers in the study above followed an ethical code.

7 Give examples of the three types of stressors investigated in the above study.

8 Explain why the researchers thought that day-to-day hassles/minor stressors might lead to ill health.

9 Explain why the researchers wanted to follow up the questionnaire study with a longitudinal study.

5 Conformity and obedience

Exercise 5A Multiple-choice questions

1 Which of the following is not a type of conformity? Choose one option only.

   a Compliance

   b Regression

   c Identification

   d Internalisation

2 Which of the following is a motivation to conform that relates to wanting to be liked and accepted by a group? Choose one option only.

   a Normative influence

   b Biased influence

   c Informational influence

   d Media influence

3 Which of the following researchers conducted a series of research studies into conformity in the 1950s during which participants had to judge lengths of lines? Choose one option only.

   a Mori

   b Sherif

   c Milgram

   d Asch

4 Which of the following makes people less likely to conform? Choose one option only.

   a Low self-esteem

   b High self-esteem

   c Authoritarian parenting

   d Democratic parenting

5 What term is used to describe cultures where family and society are valued more than individual likes and choices? Choose one option only.

   a Neoliberal

   b Socialist

   c Collectivist

   d Communist

6 Which of the following group ratios would result in the highest level of conformity among the minority group? Choose one option only.

   a A 2:1 majority

   b A 3:1 majority

   c A 3:2 majority

   d A 7:2 majority

7 Which of the following is <u>not</u> a feature of obedience? Choose one option only.

a It involves pressure from a person with more social power.
b The pressure comes from an individual rather than a group.
c It is usually prompted by a direct command.
d It usually results in the person doing the same thing as the person giving the orders.

8 Which of the following situations would lead to the lowest level of obedience, other things being equal? Choose one option only.

a The authority figure is wearing a t-shirt.
b The authority figure has left the room.
c Someone who will be harmed by an action is sitting nearby.
d A peer is refusing to obey.

9 Which of the following was a feature of the Milgram (1963) obedience experiment? Choose one option only.

a 50 participants were tested.
b It was conducted at Stanford University in California.
c Participants were told it was a 'study of memory and learning'.
d It involved people being asked to pick up litter.

10 What was the obedience rate in the original Milgram study? Choose one option only.

a 41%
b 53%
c 65%
d 79%

Exercise 5B Types of conformity and motivation to conform

1 True or false – conformity involves changing behaviour in order to come into line with orders or instructions.

2 What is meant by compliance?

3 For which two types of conformity would the behaviour continue in private (when the group was no longer present).

4 Look at the following example of social behaviour:

> Elea listens to techno music with her school friends, but when she goes to university she becomes friends with people who like rock, and starts listening to that.

Which type of conformity is being shown in the example above?

5 A person has internalised their conformity to a social group. Briefly explain what would happen to the behaviour if the group ceased to exist?

6 Why do some people who become vegetarian later conform and eat meat, while others do not?

7 Complete the following sentences:

a .... influence occurs when conformity is motivated by a desire to be right.

b .... influence occurs when conformity is motivated by a desire to be liked or to fit in with the group.

8 Decide whether each of the following examples relate to normative or informational influence:

1 Pavel is new in school. He doesn't know where to go when the morning bell rings, so he follows other pupils of his own age.

2 John notices that everyone else is eating their pizza with cutlery rather than with their hands, so he decides to do the same.

3 Bavana is unsure what to wear to a formal dinner and so she texts a couple of her friends to ask what they will be wearing.

9 Summarise one research study that demonstrated informational influence.

10 Complete the sentences by choosing the best words from the selection below. You do not have to use all the words:

75%   everyone   length   Jenness   number   Asch

A study by .... (1951) tested whether social pressure would result in people denying something they could see quite clearly with their own eyes. It tested people's judgement of the .... of lines; in a simple task, participants were asked to state which one out of three 'comparison' lines was the same as the 'standard' line. Findings showed that .... conformed on a least one occasion – demonstrating that most people are willing to say something that they know is wrong due to social pressure.

Exercise 5C Factors affecting conformity

1 Briefly described two ways in which the research of Mori and Arai (2010) differed from the research by Solomon Asch (e.g. Asch, 1951).

> **Make the link**
>
> See pages 75 & 79 for a description of the Asch, and Mori and Arai studies.

2 Look at the example below. Explain which research method is being used, and why might it have been chosen.

> A team of psychologists are investigating normative influence. They recruit participants using an advert, which states that they want to test people's ability at maths. Volunteers are then taken to a university computer room in groups of ten, and each seated at an individual computer. They are told that they have to type in answers to simple arithmetic problems such as 7×8 as they appear on the screen. The responses of the other participants in the room are displayed at the top of each person's screen. However, the researchers have manipulated the procedure to ensure that incorrect responses (apparently from the other participants) display on some of the trials, so that participants think that the other people in the room have got the answer wrong. The researchers then test how many people conform to these incorrect answers.

3 In the example above, what principle of research ethics has been violated?

4 In the example above, the arithmetic tasks used were fairly simple. Explain what might happen to conformity levels if very difficult maths problems were used instead.

5 What is the term for cultures that tend to value family and community ahead of individual choice?

6 Briefly explain a cultural difference in conformity.

7 Complete the following box:

Factor	Type of factor	Description
Group size	a	Larger groups increase the rate of conformity but only up to around a 3:1 majority.
Unanimity	Situational	b
c	Situational	More difficult tasks tend to lead to higher rates of conformity.
d	Individual	Females tend to conform at a higher rate than males.
Self-esteem	e	People with high self-esteem and confident personalities conform less.
Cultural background	Cultural	f

Exercise 5D Obedience

1 Give one real-world example of obedience.

2 Look at the following example of social behaviour:

> Socialisation means the way that our upbringing in a particular society and culture affects our later behaviour. Children learn what is expected of them, adopting many of the society's norms. Teachers and parents play a role in telling young people what behaviour is good and expected, and what behaviour is problematic.

Briefly explain what effect socialisation can have on obedience.

> **Hint** Focus on how socialisation can change children, and how this could make them more (or less) likely to obey.

3 Describe the characteristics of authoritarian parenting.

4 Briefly explain the effect of proximity in the Milgram research.

5 Complete the sentences by choosing the best words from the selection below. You do not have to use all the words:

> **uncertain   legitimate   charismatic   perception   traditional   guesswork**

Many parts of society such as schools and workplaces are structured as hierarchies, meaning that people with lower ranks or status are expected to obey those in higher positions. These people in higher positions are seen as having .... authority – they have the right to tell others what to do.

Sometimes, however, the legitimacy of an authority figure is not clear – someone may give an order, but people are not sure whether to obey. This is because legitimacy is a matter of ...., and will depend on the specific situation a person is in.

Legitimate authority is sometimes seen as deriving from one of three sources: traditional authority, legal authority and charismatic authority. A .... authority figure uses personal charm and persuasion to get others to obey them. Many political rebels and religious dissidents fall into this group.

6 Evaluate the ethics of the Milgram (1963) experiment.

7 Complete the following sentences:

.... state – seeing yourself as being in power; acting on your own wishes and morals.

.... state – seeing another person as having power; acting on behalf of their principles/commands.

8 Look at the following example of social behaviour:

> Louise is a 16-year-old girl who plays as a goalkeeper. Her coach is angry at her for missing a penalty save, and tells another player, Stacey, to punch Louise. Stacey is initially unwilling to do so, but when the coach provides reassurance and promises to take full responsibility, she goes ahead and punches Louise.

Explain why Stacey obeyed, with reference to autonomous and agentic levels of behaviour.

9 Briefly explain how authoritarian parenting could influence a person's level of obedience.

10 Analyse the research evidence relating to the situational factors in obedience, including the wearing of a uniform.

11 Complete the following sentences about obedience research:

a Hofling et al. (1966) conducted an experiment in a hospital, a setting that had more .... validity than previous obedience studies.

b Bickman's (1974) study was conducted on the .... of New York.

c One of Milgram's participants .... to continue because he understood what electric shocks can do.

d Zimbardo's prison experiment also demonstrated obedience, because prisoners obeyed the .... in the study.

e The final switch on Milgram's shock apparatus was labelled: ....

12 State the overall levels of obedience in the different variations of Milgram's study in the following diagram. They are already in the correct order from the lowest to the highest obedience level.

Statement	Level of obedience (%)
Peers rebel: two confederate teachers both disobeyed at specific points (150V and 210V).	a
Remote authority: the authority figure gave initial instructions and then left the room.	b
Touch proximity: the teacher had to hold the learner's hand down to receive a 'shock'.	c
Proximity: the teacher was in the same room as the learner.	d
Peers rebel: a confederate teacher pressed the switches, so that the true participant only had to read the questions.	e

Exercise 5E Extended scenario

Look at the following example of social behaviour, and answer the questions that follow:

Ben is a new science teacher who has started working in a small Scottish secondary school. He has noticed that pupils are less well behaved when he is leading the class compared to the more experienced teachers in the department. He asks for feedback from the head of department, who tells him that his lessons are very well-organised and that he teaches well, and says that it's probably just inevitable that a newer teacher will receive less respect.

Ben isn't satisfied with this response, and he decides to read some books about obedience and pupil behaviour. He comes across social psychology research which suggests that several factors affect obedience. Some that appear to be relevant are the presence or absence of an authority figure, and the role of agentic and autonomous behaviour. He reads up on different types of power, and on how obedience changes in group settings.

The following week, Ben takes a different approach to his lessons. He ensures that he gives instructions to the most obedient pupils first, and does not give pupils an opportunity to discuss how to respond. He stands very close when speaking to the pupils, and refers to himself as a 'fully qualified teacher' and an 'expert in his field'. He also wears his smartest and most formal clothes.

1 Briefly explain what is meant by a perceived legitimate authority figure.

2 Pupils were behaving less well for Ben than for the other teachers in the department.

   a Briefly explain one factor in obedience that could affect this.

   b Explain one factor in obedience that is <u>not</u> responsible for this difference.

> **Hint** For (b) consider a factor in obedience that didn't change. What things are the same for both Ben and the other teachers?

3 Briefly explain <u>two</u> factors affecting obedience which Ben finds out about.

> **Hint** If you are unsure, write a list of all of the situational and individual factors in obedience that you have studied, then consider each one in turn to see whether it links to the scenario.

4 Explain why Ben gives instructions to the most obedient pupils first, and avoids giving them the chance to discuss these.

Exercise 5F Integrating research understanding

Look at the following research study into social behaviour, and answer the questions that follow.

A researcher is conducting an observation study of conformity. She gains permission to observe children during lunchtimes at a local primary school. In preparation for the study, she arranges for a parental information sheet about the study to be sent home in the schoolbag of every child.

The aim of the research is to find out about how conformity changes as children get older. To do this, the researcher aims to focus on two groups of children in particular – Primary 1 and Primary 4. She reviews previous studies of playground behaviour, and prepares an observation schedule, which lists likely behaviours. She gets class lists and photographs from the school, allowing her to identify the ages of the children she observes.

Data is gathered over three days. On the first day, the researcher sits at the school office, using her observation schedule to observe any children who choose not to go outside. On the second day, she sits on a bench in the playground and watches children who are outside. Then, on the third day, she arranges for the children to play a competitive board game involving general knowledge, which is played in teams of four. She is interested in whether this will lead, on occasion, to pupils conforming to the rest of their group and giving a wrong answer.

When the data are analysed, the researcher finds that conformity is at quite a high level among the Primary 1 boys, but falls as they get older. Among the girls, conformity levels start slightly lower, but then stay at the same level across the two age groups.

1. What research method was used in the example above? What differences were there between the three days of the study, and how might this affect data?

2. What is an observation schedule?

3. Give one example of a behaviour that could appear on the researcher's observation schedule.

4. What sampling technique was used in the study, and how might this have affected results?

5. Why did the researcher arrange for pupils to play the game in groups of four?

6. Explain the changes to conformity levels that can occur as people get older, with reference to research evidence.

7. Pupils might conform for various reasons during the group task. Briefly explain one reason why a pupil might be motivated to change their answer and conform to the rest of their group.

8. What effect on conformity might it have if a pupil has higher self-esteem than their peers?

6 Prejudice

Exercise 6A Multiple-choice questions

1 What type of discrimination is occurring when someone well qualified is denied a job because the employer would prefer a younger candidate? Choose one option only.

   a Sexism

   b Racism

   c Ageism

   d Heterosexism

2 Which of the following is <u>not</u> an aspect of intergroup bias? Choose one option only.

   a Cognitive

   b Behavioural

   c Spiritual

   d Affective

3 Which of the following is an example of the behavioural aspect of prejudice? Choose one option only.

   a Attacking someone from an ingroup.

   b Paying someone from an outgroup less money than an equivalent ingroup worker.

   c Hating people from an outgroup.

   d Believing that people from an outgroup are lazy.

4 Which of the following is an example of indirect discrimination? Choose one option only.

   a A job requires working hours that are impossible if you have children.

   b A tourist is not allowed to visit a country because of his religion.

   c A new employee is denied promotion because he's too young.

   d A woman is denied a job because she is pregnant.

5 Which of the following is one problem associated with stereotyping? Choose one option only.

   a A stereotype is a type of schema, and therefore inaccurate.

   b Stereotypes prompt people to compete over resources.

   c Stereotypes usually lead to violent behaviour.

   d Even if broadly true, the stereotype might not apply to a specific person.

6 Which of the following is <u>not</u> a characteristic of people with authoritarian personalities as described by Adorno et al. (1950)? Choose one option only.

   a Conventional values.

   b A tendency to think in rigid categories.

   c More likely to rebel against authority.

   d Condemnation of minority groups.

7 What participants did Tajfel (1970) use in his minimal groups experiment? Choose one option only.

a School pupils

b Office workers

c Students

d Taxi drivers

8 Which of the following statements best summarises the main finding of Tajfel (1970)?

a Participants always picked the best reward for their own group.

b Participants ensured their own group got a better reward than the other group, even if it meant getting less overall.

c Participants always chose the fairest option overall.

d Participants only favoured their own group if they were reminded about a stereotype.

9 Which of the following terms is associated with realistic conflict theory? Choose one option only.

a Stereotype threat

b Right-wing authoritarianism

c Social categorisation

d Superordinate goals

10 Which of the following research studies was <u>not</u> conducted on school children? Choose one option only.

a Elliott's blue eyes–brown eyes exercise

b Sherif's 'Robber's Cave' study

c Paluck's radio study of attitudes in Rwanda

d Aronson and Bridgeman's jigsaw technique research

Exercise 6B Prejudice and discrimination

1 Complete the following sentences:

a Prejudice is an .... , usually negative, towards another person based on their perceived membership of a group.

b An ingroup is a group that we consider ourselves to be a member of; other groups are known as ....

2 Look at the following example of social behaviour:

> Duncan is a doctor. He is at a party where he doesn't know anyone. He chooses to sit at a table with a group of other doctors, rather than with nurses or politicians.

Briefly explain the example in terms of Duncan's ingroup and outgroups.

3 Explain the difference between direct and indirect discrimination, with examples.

> Hint For examples of indirect discrimination, there is no direct rule harming a group – instead, it is the effects of a rule that unfairly harm some groups more than others.

4 Briefly explain the connection between schemas and stereotypes.

5 Complete the following box:

Type of discrimination	Description
Racism	a
b	Discrimination against someone on the basis of their biological sex or perceived gender identity.
Ageism	c

6 What groups can experience prejudice and discrimination, besides the victims of racism/ageism/sexism?

7 Tick the statements that are true in the following.

Statement	True or False
Stereotypes are easily changed.	
Being reminded of a negative stereotype can lead to doing worse on a task.	
Films and books often include stereotyped characters.	
Some stereotypes are shown as young as age 2.	
Most psychologists think that stereotypes use up extra mental resources such as attention.	

8 Look at the example below. Briefly explain the variables under investigation:

Dr Aitken and Dr Freeman are conducting a research study into prejudice. They have hypothesised that people's choice of media (tabloid newspaper, TV news, etc) will affect their prejudice level towards outgroup members. They divide a group of participants according to their main way of consuming news. They then test participants on a standard computerised test of prejudice. In order to avoid distractions, they conduct the study in a noise-proof room with no windows.

Exercise 6C Explanations of prejudice

1 Complete the sentences by choosing the best words from the selection below. You do not have to use all the words.

> independently   assumptions   automatically   stereotypes   shortcut   effort

Cognitive miser theory is an explanation of why people hold stereotypes, based on cognitive limitations. It states that a stereotype is a mental .... , made because people cannot or do not wish to make the mental effort to process each person's traits individually. Some researchers believe that we make simplifying .... about people and situations all of the time, and we would be unable to operate without them. This view implies that a lot of our thinking and decision making happens largely ...., without intention or conscious awareness.

2 Complete the following sentences about three traits of people with authoritarian personalities:

Conventionalism involves strongly subscribing to .... social values.

Authoritarian .... is a submissive attitude to power and authority.

Authoritarian .... is a hatred and rejection of minorities.

3 Explain the processes involved in developing an authoritarian personality.

> **Hint** Think about the childhood processes involved. Make the link to psychoanalytic theory.

4 What questionnaire was used in the early research into authoritarian personality theory?

5 Briefly explain what is meant by a person's 'social identity'.

6 Look at the following example of social behaviour:

> Ady is a 10-year-old boy. When walking to school in the morning, he chats and walks along with Jenna, a girl from his class who lives nearby. However, when he gets to school he never chooses to spend time with Jenna, and only talks to male classmates when in the playground.

With reference to social identity theory, explain why Ady is happy to spend time with female friends out of school but not in the school setting.

7 Briefly explain the main principle behind realistic conflict theory.

8 Explain the methodology of Sherif et al.'s (1954) 'Robber's Cave' experiment.

9 What prejudiced behaviour does realistic conflict theory not explain?

> **🔍 Top tip**
>
> Take note of situations where the explanations of prejudice say different things, or where one is better at explaining a situation than another. These points can be used to analyse the theories.

> **Make the link**
>
> See page 92 for a description of the Sherif et al (1954) study.

10 Which of the following groups have been victims of scapegoating?

- Ethnic minorities
- Colleagues
- Religious minorities
- Teenagers
- Working mothers
- Homosexual people

11 What cognitive process could maintain and strengthen the process of scapegoating?

12 Briefly summarise the evidence for scapegoat theory.

> Hint Evidence relating to biases and stereotypes can be applied to scapegoating.

Exercise 6D Reducing prejudice

1 Complete the sentences by choosing the best words from the selection below. You do not have to use all the words.

> eye   favourite   threat   distress   fear   awareness

Education involves tackling the cognitive aspect of prejudice, and occurs in schools or other educational settings. Its main aims are to raise .... about stereotypes, and to teach strategies that tackle prejudiced thinking. Jane Elliott devised an educational technique where .... colour is used to determine how people were treated, allowing everyone to understand what it felt like to be the victim of discrimination. School children labelled inferior on the basis of their eye colour did worse at a card-sorting task, suggesting that stereotype .... could have an immediate impact on school performance. However, the technique is confrontational and caused some .... among the children.

2 True or false: when affirmative action is used, jobs are always given to minorities.

3 Look at the following example of social behaviour:

> Jasmine is running a new drama class. Each member of the class will take part in a project in two parts: first working on developing characters, and then write writing and performing a short play. However, the class are ethnically diverse and don't know each other very well. She decides to use the jigsaw technique.

Explain how the jigsaw technique would be used in this situation.

4 Briefly describe one example of how the media can challenge stereotypes.

5 Give an example of affirmative action.

6 What term is used to describe the type of goals that help bring conflicting groups together?

Exercise 6E Extended scenario

1 Look at the following example of social behaviour, and answer the questions that follow:

> Ashleigh is a 3rd year school pupil. She is on a school trip to the Speyside area of Scotland, an area of natural beauty that is also noted for its whisky industry. The pupils are accompanied by their Music teacher and their Science teacher. These are Ashleigh's two favourite subjects; she is very good at both science and music, but is struggling to decide which of them she wishes to pursue as a career.
>
> One day on the trip, Ashleigh's teachers lead a tour around a whisky distillery, and Ashleigh asks a lot of questions about the process involved in distilling alcohol. Her Science teacher suggests that she should consider becoming a scientist one day, saying that she is a hardworking girl and clearly interested in chemical processes. However, her Music teacher suggests that girls are not naturally suited to science careers, and that perhaps she should focus her efforts on her musical talent instead.
>
> Later Ashleigh and her friends are asked to divide themselves into groups for a game of baseball, and each teacher acts as a team captain. The teachers suggest that the teams be named after their subjects, Team Science and Team Music. Ashleigh is randomly picked to be on Team Science. As the game progresses, the pupils begin to get very competitive about the game, and start to call each other names. Ashleigh finds herself hating Team Music. The next day she tells her friends that she doesn't even like Music as a subject.

a Briefly explain what is meant by sexism.

b i Briefly explain what is meant by a stereotype.

  ii Give an example of a stereotype from the scenario above.

  iii Explain how the messages Ashleigh receives from her teachers could link to the concepts of stereotype threat and stereotype lift.

c Explain the scenario in terms of social identity theory, <u>or</u> another explanation of prejudice.

> **Hint** Focus on social identity or realistic conflict theory. Pick whichever one you understand best.

Exercise 6F Integrating research understanding

1 Look at the following example of research into social behaviour:

> A university-based researcher plans to investigate the effect of the media on stereotypes. She decides to show one of her classes of students a TV show for half an hour a week, over four weeks, pretending that it is part of their class on social behaviour. She has chosen the show as it has strongly sexist and homophobic characters. She then plans to test the students' level of prejudice, using another class as a control group.

Should the research example above by approved by the university's ethics board?

Look at the following research study into social behaviour, and answer the questions that follow.

A researcher, Dr Kynaston, is conducting a field experiment relating to prejudice. He used random sampling to select several UK primary schools, and then approached each school to find out if they were willing to take part in his study.

The research study involves dividing pupils into two groups according to their type of hair – straight hair or curly hair. Pupils with one hair type will be given special privileges, and the researcher will use teacher accomplices to record what effect this has on pupils' work rate. In particular, he thinks that pupils who are placed in a situation of stereotype threat will be less motivated, and so will work less quickly.

Dr Kynaston is sure that this is an innovative study that has never been done before. In order to avoid extraneous variables, the study keeps certain aspects of the procedure the same for all participants. The testing is to be done first thing on a Monday morning, and should last for two hours. Schools are also given access to a short film, which can be shown to pupils as a debriefing.

Disappointingly, a large number of the schools that he initially approached refused to take part. Some told Dr Kynaston that this will be distressing for pupils, and others do not want children to focus on aspects of each other's appearance in case it leads to bullying. Some schools have simply said that they are too busy covering the curriculum to take part in a research project.

2 Describe the main features of field experiments.

3 Explain <u>one</u> reason why a field experiment is a suitable research method with which to investigate the issue described above.

4 a Explain what is meant by an independent variable and a dependent variable.
   b Identify the IV and DV in the study above.

5 Explain why the IV in the study above might affect pupils' behaviour or work rate. Refer to research in your answer.

6 Explain what is meant by an extraneous variable, and give an example.

7 Some researchers have used the jigsaw technique to reduce conflict and prejudice in classrooms. Briefly explain how the jigsaw technique is set up.

8 Explain why the following ethical considerations are important in research:

   a Informed consent
   b Confidentiality

9 Briefly explain one thing that Dr Kynaston could do to improve his research study.

7 Social relationships

Exercise 7A Multiple-choice questions

1 What is a broad term meaning the desire to form relationships with other people, which could be due to liking, to attraction, or for strategic reasons? Choose one option only.

   a Bonding

   b Affiliation

   c Attachment

   d Comparison

2 Which of the following concepts describes how people tend to form romantic relationships with others of similar attractiveness level to themselves? Choose one option only.

   a The chameleon effect

   b Costs and benefits

   c Parental investment

   d The matching hypothesis

3 Which of the following is the term used for the way we judge future relationships based on past experience? Choose one answer only.

   a Cortisol

   b Comparison level

   c Bargaining

   d Break-ups

4 Which of the following happens during the commitment stage of a relationship, according to social exchange theory?

   a Costs are lowered

   b Costs increase

   c A new relationship is formed

   d A relationship breaks up

5 According to the evolutionary theory of relationships, what relationship behaviour is similar for both males and females? Choose one option only.

   a They are motivated to avoid being cheated on.

   b They try to have as many children as possible.

   c They are usually attracted to individuals younger than themselves.

   d They avoid having romantic relationships at all.

6 What is Dunbar's number? Choose one option only.

   a 50

   b 100

   c 150

   d 200

7 Which of the following is <u>not</u> a filter used during relationship choice? Choose one option only.

a Proximity

b Compatible views

c Availability to enter a relationship

d Investment

8 Which of the following is <u>not</u> a factor in whether a relationship is maintained, according to Rusbult's theory? Choose one option only.

a Duration of relationship

b Comparison with alternatives

c Investment size

d Satisfaction level

9 Which of the following is <u>not</u> one of the levels of parasocial relationships described by Giles and Maltby (2006)? Choose one option only.

a Entertainment-social

b Intense-personal

c Borderline pathological

d Neurotic-imaginative

10 Which of the following can act as a gating feature in relationship formation? Choose one option only.

a Shyness

b Food preferences

c Online dating

d Hair colour

Exercise 7B Defining relationships

1 Complete the following sentences:

a The term 'relationship' has a .... definition in Psychology, including connections with friends, colleagues, and even enemies.

b Researchers such as Maslow have argued that relationships are a basic human ....

c Affiliation means the desire to form connections with other people to avoid social isolation or for .... reasons.

2 Look at the following example of social behaviour:

Clare is a politician from a small Scottish political party. At a committee in parliament, she circulates and speaks to several members of other parties. She dislikes some of them intensely, but is polite and tries to make constructive arguments about an upcoming vote. There are a few rivals who she always enjoys talking to – even though they differ on politics, she finds them funny and good to talk to.

Briefly explain the example in terms of affiliation and attraction.

3 Briefly explain what is meant by the matching hypothesis.

4 Look at the example below. Briefly explain the variables under investigation:

> Dr Zarrug and Dr McCullagh are conducting a research study into relationships. They have hypothesised that religious affiliation will show matching, with people more attracted to others of the same religious views as themselves. They divide a group of participants according to their religious views as stated on a recruitment interview, taking into account three major religions plus a non-religious group. They then test participants on a computerised test that shows faces together with (fictitious) information about the person's name and religious beliefs. Participants are asked to rate each face for attractiveness. In order to avoid distractions, the researchers conduct the study in a noise-proof room with no windows.

Exercise 7C Theories of relationships

1 Tick those of the following statements that are true of social exchange theory.

Statement	True or False
According to Thibaut and Kelley, a relationship involves a series of social exchanges between partners.	
Each partner gets a bad deal from every social exchange.	
Every individual will try to minimise their costs, and get as much benefit as possible out of the relationship.	
Having a high level of costs and a low level of benefits will lead to a person being more likely to form or maintain a relationship.	

2 Give an example of a cost in a relationship.

3 Complete the following sentences about the four relationship stages described by social exchange theory.

.... is where a person considers costs and rewards on offer, and compares other potential relationships.

.... is where a new couple give and receive rewards, e.g. gifts, and consider whether deeper commitment is worthwhile.

.... is where a relationship becomes more predictable and costs are lowered as the bond and commitment increases over time.

.... is where norms are established in the pattern of exchange within the relationship.

4 Complete the sentences by choosing the best words from the selection below. You do not have to use all the words.

> 25%   50%   parental   advisor   carer   shortcut   investment

Evolutionary theories of relationships focus on .... investment – the idea that for biological reasons, males and females invest different amounts of resources in having and raising children. Some researchers argue that these differences have led the two sexes to evolve different behavioural strategies. Both parents have the same genetic stake in the child's survival, as every child gets .... of its genes from each parent. However, the costs to the two parents differ. Even in societies that have relatively equal roles for males and females, females put in a greater biological investment, through pregnancy and breastfeeding. This differential is increased if the mother is also the primary .... for her offspring. Another sex difference is that women can have fewer offspring over the course of their lives than a man can.

5 Complete the following box, identifying whether each feature is considered an innate factor affecting attraction or not:

Aspect of appearance/attraction	Innate or not?
Preference for healthy skin tone	a
What clothes people wear	b
A preference for symmetrical faces	c

6 Briefly summarise the evidence for relationship behaviour being innate.

> Hint | Evidence for innate (rather than learned) attachment behaviour in childhood can be used as supporting evidence, but romantic relationships should also be included.

7 Explain the processes involved in relationship choice according to filter theory.

> Hint | Give supporting research evidence and examples.

8 Briefly explain how Rusbult's investment theory helps us to understand harmful relationships.

9 Briefly explain how the roles of relationship equity, investment and a shared social network can change over time.

10 Look at the following example of social behaviour:

> Nadia is a 20-year-old student. She has met another girl from her class who lives nearby.

With reference to any theory of relationships, explain whether Nadia and her classmate are likely to form a relationship.

Exercise 7D Virtual and parasocial relationships

1 Complete the following sentence:

A .... relationship involves using the internet to meet potential partners and/or maintain a relationship.

2 Briefly explain the main principle behind gating features in online relationships.

3 Explain the similarities between child–parent attachment bonds and later romantic relationships.

4 What term is used by Walther to describe online communication that is deep and personal, and allows people to fulfil their goals?

5 Explain Walther's reduced cues theory.

> **Hint** Consider both the differences (online vs. face-to-face communication) and the effects of these differences.

6 Explain the findings of the Walther et al. (2018) 'message persistence' experiment.

> **Make the link**
>
> See page 107 for a description of the Walther et al. research.

7 Does the internet only have an effect on new relationships?

8 Complete the sentences by choosing the best words from the selection below. You do not have to use all the words.

> adolescents   computer   attachments   unaware   celebrity   appreciative

A parasocial relationship is a one-sided relationship between an ordinary individual and a .... This relationship is stronger and more intense than the behaviour of a typical fan and may be seen as a crush or obsession, while the celebrity in question is typically .... of the person's feelings. Individuals who are engaged in parasocial relationships may feel as if they know the celebrity, and often research them in a huge amount of detail. Parasocial relationships are more commonly found among .... , perhaps because they have not yet developed a fully mature social network. Parasocial relationships are more likely to occur when the celebrity and their fan have similar values, and may link to an individual's other .... , e.g. to their friends or parents – intense personal interest in celebrities appears to be connected to low levels of closeness to parents.

9 Briefly explain what is meant by the 'borderline pathological' level of parasocial relationships.

10 True or false: there is a risk that parasocial relationships can lead to eating disorders and poor mental health.

11 Briefly describe the main principle of the absorption-addiction model of parasocial relationships.

12 Look at the following example of social behaviour:

> Calum is a psychologist who is running a weekly support group for vulnerable and isolated adults. He finds that the group members are quite poor at forming new interpersonal relationships, and at judging who they might share interests with. They tend to communicate with one another on quite a superficial level.

Explain how the internet could affect this situation.

Exercise 7E Extended scenario

Look at the following example of social behaviour, and answer the questions that follow:

> Emilia is a 3rd year school pupil who is obsessed with an internet celebrity called Star. She feels she has a connection with Star, and although they have never met in real life and Star has never replied to any of Emilia's messages in person, Emilia feels that they have a spiritual connection. She feels as if somehow their minds are connected, and is sure that they are destined to be together as a couple.
>
> Every time Star releases a new video, Emilia watches it several times over, and it's all she will talk about for some time after that. She tends to ask other people questions about Star's expressions and body language, and about exactly what was said in the video and what it might mean, regardless of whether others are interested in discussing this or not. If Star ever describes anything bad that has happened to her during her videos, Emilia finds herself feeling intensely anxious, and sometimes cries for hours.
>
> At school, Emilia's friends think that her obsession is a bit weird, but for the most part, it's just accepted as part of who she is. However, her closest school friends notice that Emilia increasingly talks as if she has a genuine relationship with Star – as if they know each other. Indeed, she talks about Star more often than she talks about her siblings or parents.

1
  a Briefly explain what is meant by a parasocial relationship.
  b Explain one or more effects that a parasocial relationship can have on the fan involved, with reference to the scenario above.
  c In the scenario above, what level of parasocial relationship does Emilia have?
  d Explain how this parasocial relationship may have developed, with reference to at least one theory.

Exercise 7F Integrating research understanding

1 Look at the following example of research into social behaviour:

> A university-based researcher plans to investigate the effect of the media on relationships. She decides to show one of her classes of students a TV show for half an hour a week, over four weeks, pretending that it is part of their class on social behaviour. She has chosen a TV show that features a number of dysfunctional and abusive romantic relationships. She then plans to test the students' attitudes about what circumstances should lead to a couple breaking up, using another class as a control group.

Should the research example above by approved by the university's ethics board?

Look at the following research study into social behaviour, and answer the questions that follow.

A postgraduate psychology researcher, Nalini, is conducting a field experiment relating to relationships. She used random sampling to select several universities around the country, and then approached each one to find out if they were willing to take part in her study. If they agree, she puts up a notice asking for volunteer participants.

The research study involves placing first-year undergraduates into a situation where they meet somebody new via a computer, and then finding out how likeable and attractive they find that person. Participants are randomly paired up, and given a task where they ask each other questions on a laptop while sitting in different rooms of the university library. In one condition they are given a list of questions that are detailed and concern a person's values and attitudes, while in the other condition they are given questions that are all very superficial and concern what the person did yesterday. Participants do not see each other's physical appearance. Nalini has hypothesised that how students react will depend on signs of compatibility, with those who ask questions about values more likely to state that they found the other person likeable and attractive.

In order to avoid extraneous variables, the study keeps certain aspects of the procedure the same for all participants. Every pair of participants is tested at 9 a.m. The procedure is always stopped after 20 minutes, after which a short debriefing video automatically starts to play on the laptop.

Disappointingly, a large number of the universities that Nalini initially approached refused to take part. Some told her that this research will distract students from their work, and others are worried that if the experiment leads to new romantic relationships forming, they will be morally responsible for anything harmful that happens at a later point. Some universities have simply said that they are too busy to organise time and space in the library for the study to take place.

2 Describe the main features of field experiments.

3 Is a field experiment a suitable research method with which to investigate the issue described above? Explain one relevant issue.

4 a Explain what is meant by an independent variable and a dependent variable.

b Identify the IV and DV in the study above.

5 Explain why the IV in the study above might affect attraction. Refer to research in your answer.

6 Explain what is meant by an extraneous variable, and give an example.

7 Some researchers have studied the effect of the internet on relationships. Explain how the internet might affect the formation or maintenance of relationships.

8 Explain why the following ethical considerations are important in research:

a Informed consent

b Confidentiality

9 Briefly explain one thing that Nalini could do to improve her research study.

8 Aggression

Exercise 8A Multiple-choice questions

1 What type of aggression is involved if a person refuses to speak to someone they are annoyed with? Choose one option only.

   a Impulsive aggression

   b Instrumental aggression

   c Sanctioned aggression

   d Passive aggression

2 Which area of the brain is associated with fear and aggression? Choose one option only.

   a The amygdala

   b The hypothalamus

   c The corpus callosum

   d The cerebellum

3 Which of the following is a hormone that is associated with aggression? Choose one option only.

   a Testosterone

   b GABA

   c Cortisol

   d Melatonin

4 Which of the following is an example of 'mate-guarding'? Choose one option only.

   a Animals fighting before winning a mate.

   b Birds who have formed mating pairs fighting off their rivals.

   c People staying in a lifelong relationship.

   d Having more than one boyfriend or girlfriend.

5 Which term refers to the process of genes being switched off or on depending on the environment? Choose one option only.

   a MAOA

   b Epigenetics

   c Nature-nurture

   d Innate aggression

6 Which of the following is the ethological term for patterns of behaviours such as aggressive actions? Choose one option only.

   a Limbic systems

   b Imprinting

   c Fixed action patterns

   d Releasers

7 In which species of fish did Tinbergen (1952) study aggressive acts related to mating and territory? Choose one option only.

a Cod

b Stickleback

c Sardine

d Shark

8 Which of the following was <u>not</u> one of the factors identified by Sykes (1958) as something that prisoners were deprived of? Choose one option only.

a Liberty

b Autonomy

c Wi-fi

d Goods

9 Which of the following is <u>not</u> one of the prison sub-cultures described by Irwin and Cressey (1962)?

a Thief sub-culture

b Legitimate sub-culture

c Convict sub-culture

d Mafia sub-culture

10 Which of the following is <u>not</u> one of the findings of Bandura's research into social learning of aggression among children? Choose one option only.

a Children were more likely to imitate realistic violence.

b There was more imitation of an adult of their own sex.

c Children imitated verbal aggression.

d No aggression was shown unless there was a reward.

Exercise 8B Defining aggression

1 Complete the following sentence:

a Aggression can be defined as any .... harmful act towards another member of the same species.

b Impulsive aggressive acts are .... and focused on another individual, with the aim of harming them.

c Instrumental aggression is a means to an end or aims to obtained a desired ..../ for example to scare someone off or steal something .

2 Look at the following example of social behaviour:

> Keir is an S5 school pupil. He is discussing moving away from home. His mother says that he is too young, and needs to wait until the end of sixth year. Keir rolls his eyes, says 'fine', and then walks out of the room, slamming the door behind him.

Briefly explain the example in terms of aggression and passive aggression.

3 Look at the example below. Briefly explain the variables under investigation:

Dr Haughton and Dr Ahrens are conducting a research study into aggression. They have hypothesised that people who are frustrated at work will show more instrumental aggression. They divide volunteers according to their self-reported level of workplace frustration, and then administer a standard computerised test of instrumental aggression. In order to avoid distractions, they conduct the study in a noise-proof room with no windows.

Exercise 8C Biological explanations of aggression

1 Briefly explain two differences between evolutionary and ethological explanations of aggression.

2 Tick those of the following statements that are true.

Statement	True or False
Evolutionary psychology is the application of Darwin's theory of natural selection as it applies to human behaviour.	
Baboon males show high levels of aggression, with those that are victorious in fights becoming the dominant male in their tribe.	
Primate species with less sexual dimorphism (males and females are physically similar) show more aggression.	
Aggression can occur within social interactions such as via gossip, and links to people trying to establish a better place within a social hierarchy.	
Evolutionary psychologists agree that individuals will always act to help their species survive, even if this kills them or prevents them from raising offspring	

3 Explain the evolutionary approach to aggression.

Hint | Consider the basic principles of this approach. Refer to evidence from both humans and other species.

4 Complete the following box:

Concept	Description
Amygdala	a
Serotonin	b
MAOA	c

5 Briefly explain epigenetics.

6 Briefly explain the evidence for the role of the MAOA-L gene in aggression.

> **Make the link**
>
> See page 113 for a description of this research.

7 Complete the sentences by choosing the best words from the selection below. You do not have to use all the words.

> Tinbergen releasers Skinner bees action ants violence

The field of ethology is based on the work of three European researchers. Karl von Frisch discovered that .... communicate with each other by doing a 'waggle dance' when they return to their hive after discovering flowers that contain nectar. Konrad Lorenz argued that most animals have innate .... that bring a fight to an end, and suggested that humans may have lost this trait, leading to violence that doesn't stop. Niko .... was interested in how animals establish a territory, and show aggression when this is invaded by other individuals. His classic study of stickleback fish demonstrated how fixed .... patterns relating to mating and aggression are prompted by releasers that the experimenters were able to mimic. His research showed very little real fighting among the fish, indicating that their aggression was largely a form of ritual.

Exercise 8D Psychological explanations of aggression

1 Complete the following sentences about social learning theory:
* Social learning theory explains behaviour primarily in terms of learning through experience, but recognises that people make mental .... of actions.
* It states that people learn not just from the results of their own actions but also by what happens to .... around them – 'observational learning'.
* A key principle of the theory is that we don't imitate behaviour for no reason – instead, it has to be seen to be ....

2 What term means learning from others rather than through your own experience?

3 Explain the procedure of the study of imitation of aggression by Bandura, Ross and Ross (1963).

> **Make the link**
>
> See page 117 for a description of the Bandura et al. research.

4 In Bandura's research, what was the effect of unrealistic 'cartoon' violence?

5 Briefly explain the main principle behind the importation model of prison aggression.

> Hint | In this and similar questions, try to briefly capture a single main principle that sums up a theory.

6 Briefly explain the main conclusion drawn by Zimbardo and colleagues from their Stanford prison experiment.

7 What term is used to mean adopting the expectations of your social role, as was seen in the Stanford prison experiment?

8 Look at the following example of social behaviour:

> Sahar has joined a group of sports fans who travel around to many cities to visit events. Some of the group have previously spent time in prison, and show a strong sense of the importance of being tough and avoiding being controlled by others. Some of the group are highly aggressive when faced with rival groups of fans, and Sahar has started to adopt the same group norms.

With reference to one or more social-psychological explanations of aggression, explain why Sahar's group are aggressive.

Exercise 8E Media influences on aggression

1 Briefly explain the cognitive priming explanation of the role of media in aggression.

2 Which of the following studies provide evidence for the cognitive priming explanation of aggression? Identify all that apply.

- Bushman's (1998) study showing that people who had watched a violent video clip were more likely to make aggression-based word associations.
- The study that found no increase in aggression on the island of St Helena after TV was introduced.
- The Williams (1986) study of TV availability in a remote region of Canada.
- Tinbergen's (1952) study of aggression in sticklebacks.
- Bandura et al.'s (1963) study relates to the effects of TV on aggression, so is also a suitable key study when discussing media influences on aggression.
- Anderson and Dill's (2000) study of computer games and aggression.

3 Explain the methodology of Anderson and Dill's (2000) study of computer games and aggression.

 Make the link

See page 121 for a description of Anderson and Dill's research.

4 Briefly evaluate the Anderson and Dill (2000) study.

5 Briefly summarise the evidence for the role of computer games in aggressive behaviour.

> Hint | Consider the strengths of the evidence, and don't forget to include possible positive beneficial effects on behaviour.

6 Complete the sentences by choosing the best words from the selection below. You do not have to use all the words.

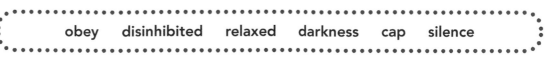

> **obey   disinhibited   relaxed   darkness   cap   silence**

Often, we are inhibited from acting in a particular way due to social norms or potential consequences of our actions. It's possible that in computer games or other online contexts, people feel .... due to the distance of buffer that exists between their actions and any potential harm that they cause. This has been observed in the context of a baiting by a crowd – it is more likely to occur in large crowds and in conditions of ...., suggested that anonymity plays a role in the behaviour. When anonymous, our motivation to follow social norms such as politeness reduces, and some of our more aggressive and selfish urges start to reveal themselves. People are also more likely to .... a harmful order.

7 True or false: disinhibition could be a factor affecting the behaviour of online 'trolls'.

8 Look at the following example of social behaviour:

> Amy is running an after-school psychology club for primary school children. She allows the children to play online video games for the first 10 minutes while their classmates arrive from different areas of the school campus. Once everyone has arrived, Amy switches off all of the computers. Some of the children react with anger and annoyance at this, shouting at Amy and pretending to fire guns at her.

Explain why the children in Amy's club may have behaved aggressively, with reference to one or more media influences on aggression.

Exercise 8F Extended scenario

Look at the following example of social behaviour, and answer the questions that follow:

> Katy is a 5th year school pupil who looks after her younger brother, Lauchlan, age 7, when he gets home from school. As she has a lot of homework to do, Katy lets her brother watch cartoons for a couple of hours. Sometimes the cartoons are very violent, she realises, but it doesn't seem to be doing much harm.
>
> One day, two of Lauchlan's friends, also boys, come home from school with him, and they all watch cartoons together. The cartoons feature superhero cats who fight each other with swords. After they have finished watching an episode, the boys find some sticks in the garden and start to play a game that involves pretending that the sticks are swords, and fighting with them. One of the boys gets hurt and cries, and Katy then gives them all cookies to cheer them up.
>
> They sit inside for a while eating cookies, until one of Lauchlan's friends realises that Katy has eaten the last cookie from the plate. The boy picks up the plate and smashes it on the ground in a rage, and then picks up his stick and hits Katy with it.

1 Briefly explain what is meant by impulsive aggression.

2 Explain a biological factor that can make males more prone to aggression than girls.

3 Explain how the media could have affected behaviour in the scenario above.

4 Explain the role of rewards in social learning theory, with reference to the scenario above.

Exercise 8G Integrated research understanding

1 Look at the following example of research into social behaviour:

> A university-based researcher plans to investigate the effect of the media on aggression. She decides to show one of her classes of students a TV show for half an hour a week, over four weeks, pretending that it is part of their class on social behaviour. She has chosen the show as it features high levels of verbal aggression. She then plans to test the students' level of aggression experimentally, using another class as a control group.

Should the research example above by approved by the university's ethics board?

Look at the following research study into social behaviour, and answer the questions that follow.

> A researcher, Professor Rosenthal, is conducting a field experiment relating to aggression. She used random sampling to select several UK primary schools, and then approached each school to find out if they were willing to take part in her study.
>
> The research involves dividing young school pupils into two groups. One group are shown a video in which a game of hockey descends into a fight, and are then given a chance to play hockey themselves. The second group of pupils are instead shown a simple video about the rules of the game, and then given the same opportunity to play hockey. Professor Rosenthal has spent many years doing research into cognitive priming, and she thinks that prior exposure to media aggression will lead to more fights breaking out among the pupils. In particular, she thinks that pupils who have watched the fight video will initiate violence if something happens during the match that makes them feel frustrated. Professor Rosenthal is sure that this is an innovative study that has never been done before.
>
> In order to avoid extraneous variables, the study keeps certain aspects of the procedure the same for all participants in the different schools. The procedure has to be followed first thing on a Monday morning, and should last for one hour including both video and hockey game. The same rules are followed for all games. Schools are also given PowerPoint slides that can be shown to classes of pupils as a debriefing.
>
> Disappointingly, a large number of the schools that she initially approached refused to take part. Some told Professor Rosenthal that this will be stressful for pupils, and others do not want to run a task that could prompt aggression in case any children get hurt. Some schools have simply said that they are too busy covering the curriculum to take part in a research project.

2 Describe the main features of field experiments.

3 Explain <u>one</u> reason why a field experiment is a suitable research method with which to investigate the issue described above.

4 a Explain what is meant by an independent variable and a dependent variable.

b Identify the IV and DV in the study above.

5 Explain why the IV in the study above might affect pupils' level of aggression. Refer to research in your answer.

6 Explain what is meant by an extraneous variable, and give an example.

7 Some researchers have tried to investigate media violence by studying aggression levels in an area that gains access to TV for the first time. Explain how such a study could be set up.

8 Explain why the following ethical considerations are important in research:

a Informed consent

b Confidentiality

9 Briefly explain one thing that Professor Rosenthal could do to improve her research study.

Part 3: Practice Test Papers

Practice exam 1

SECTION 1 — INDIVIDUAL BEHAVIOUR — 40 marks

Attempt Question 1 and ONE other from Questions 2, 3 or 4

Question 1

Individual behaviour – sleep and dreams   *Marks*

(a) Briefly explain what is meant by circadian rhythms.   **2**

(b) Evaluate Crick and Mitchison's (1986) reorganisational theory of dreaming.   **8**

(c)
> Jakub has recently been having difficulty sleeping. He speaks to his doctor, who says that Jakub should try cutting down on factors in his lifestyle and surroundings that may be making it harder for him to get to sleep.

(i)   Briefly explain two factors that affect sleep, with reference to the scenario above.   **4**

(ii) Explain one research method that could be used to investigate factors that affect sleep.   **6**

Individual behaviour – optional topic

Attempt **EITHER**

Question 2 – depression

OR

Question 3 – memory

OR

Question 4 – stress

Question 2

Individual behaviour – depression

(a) Describe major depressive disorder.   4

(b) Analyse the biological causes for depression.   10

> Andy has been feeling very down since losing a tennis match. He visits his doctor, and is referred to a cognitive behavioural therapist.

(c) Briefly describe one feature of cognitive behavioural therapy.   2

(d) Explain what is meant by the cognitive triad.   4

[Now go to Question 5]

Question 3

Individual behaviour – memory

(a) Describe the multi-store model of memory.   4

(b) Analyse the working memory model.   10

> Zenib is working on a psychology research project, and will be conducting an experiment. She is ready to gather data, but she realises that she has forgotten to print out her participant consent forms.

(c) Briefly describe one explanation for forgetting, with reference to the scenario above.   2

(d) Explain how forgetting might occur due to brain damage.   4

[Now go to Question 5]

Question 4

Individual behaviour – stress

(a) Describe the general adaptation syndrome.   4

(b) Analyse the role of hormones in stress.   10

> Philip has been walking his dog. It's raining, and he feels tired after a long day at work. As he starts to walk home, the dog barks at a group of children, and then runs away.

(c) Briefly describe one source of stress, with reference to the scenario above.   2

(d) Explain how stress might be affected by personality type.   4

[Now go to Question 5]

SECTION 2 – SOCIAL BEHAVIOUR – 40 marks

Attempt Question 5 and ONE other from Questions 6, 7 or 8

Question 5

Social behaviour – conformity and obedience

Marks

Katerina has just started a university degree in Geography. When she first starts, the other students ask her what her favourite subject at school was, and she says 'Geography' because she doesn't want to stand out from the crowd. After a few weeks, she becomes close friends with a group of fellow students who love moral philosophy. She finds herself reading books about this topic in her spare time.

(a) Explain types of conformity, with reference to the above scenario. 10

(b) Briefly describe one situational factor that affects conformity. 2

(c) Evaluate Milgram's research into obedience. 8

Social behaviour – optional topic

Attempt **EITHER**

Question 6 – prejudice

OR

Question 7 – social relationships

OR

Question 8 – aggression

Question 6

Social behaviour – prejudice

(a) Briefly explain what is meant by direct discrimination.   2

(b) Explain stereotyping.   6

> Erin is a teacher. She has noticed that the pupils in her class have formed into two groups, who prefer not to work with each other or talk to each other. One group are very interested in sports, and the other are very interested in music.

(c) Explain two ways in which prejudice can be reduced, with reference to the above scenario.   12

Question 7

Social behaviour – social relationships

(a) Briefly explain what is meant by a parasocial relationship.   2

(b) Explain the absorption-addiction model of parasocial relationships.   6

> Farid has been in a romantic relationship for several months. He lives in Scotland, and his partner lives in Italy. They get on very well and enjoy socialising with friends when they see each other, but don't share many other interests.

(c) Explain two theories of relationships, with reference to the above scenario.   12

Question 8

Social behaviour – aggression

(a) Briefly explain what is meant by aggression.   2

(b) Explain how dysfunctional institutions can affect aggression.   6

> Kennedy has been in prison for several weeks for selling drugs. At first, she didn't often speak to anyone else inside and behaved well, but recently she has found herself becoming involved in a prison riot.

(c) Explain the importation model of aggression and the deprivation model of aggression, with reference to the above scenario.   6

Practice exam 2

Duration – 2 hours 40 minutes

SECTION 1 – INDIVIDUAL BEHAVIOUR – 40 marks

Attempt Question 1 and ONE other from Questions 2, 3 or 4

Question 1

Individual behaviour – sleep and dreams   *Marks*

(a) Briefly explain what is meant by the manifest and latent content of dreams.   **2**

> Researchers have been studying Pablo, a doctor who often has to work night
> shifts. At times he sleeps overnight in the hospital where he works. However,
> he sleeps badly, waking up every hour or so. The researchers have installed
> video cameras in this hospital room in order to observe his sleep patterns.

(b) Explain ethical issues in research, with reference to the scenario above.   **4**

(c) Evaluate Czeisler et al.'s (1990) study of sleep.   **8**

(d) Explain the role of the brain in the sleep-wake cycle.   **6**

Individual behaviour – optional topic

Attempt **EITHER**

Question 2 – depression

OR

Question 3 – memory

OR

Question 4 – stress

Question 2

Individual behaviour – depression

(a) Briefly describe persistent depressive disorder.   2

(b) Explain the methods and findings of one study into the biology of depression.   8

(c) Analyse biological treatments for depression.   10

[Now go to Question 5]

Question 3

Individual behaviour – memory

(a) Briefly describe the phonological loop.   2

(b) Explain the methods and findings of one study into the working memory model.   8

(c) Analyse explanations of forgetting in long-term memory.   10

[Now go to Question 5]

Question 4

Individual behaviour – stress

(a) Briefly describe the hypothalamic–pituitary–adrenal system.   2

(b) Explain the methods and findings of one study into the physiology of stress.   8

(c) Analyse coping strategies used to tackle stress.   10

[Now go to Question 5]

SECTION 2 – SOCIAL BEHAVIOUR – 40 marks

Attempt Question 5 and ONE other from Questions 6, 7 or 8

Question 5

Social behaviour – conformity and obedience

Marks

(a) Briefly explain what is meant by perceived legitimate authority.   **2**

Thom is 14. Most of his school friends have dyed their hair. Thom does not want to do so, but he also doesn't want to be left out.

(b) Explain two or more factors that affect conformity, with reference to the above scenario.   **6**

(c) With reference to Mori and Arai's (2010) study of conformity,

    i) Evaluate the study.   **6**

    ii) Analyse the study.   **6**

Social behaviour – optional topic

Attempt **EITHER**

Question 6 – prejudice

OR

Question 7 – social relationships

OR

Question 8 – aggression

Question 6

Social behaviour – prejudice

(a) Explain what is meant by an authoritarian personality. 2

(b) Explain indirect discrimination. 4

> Mrs Knox is the chief executive of a large company. She has been criticised for the lack of diversity among her workforce, and has been meeting with her staff to discuss ways of tackling this issue.

(c) Explain how affirmative action is used to reduce prejudice, with reference to the above scenario. 6

(d) Analyse a research study that investigated ways of reducing prejudice. 8

Question 7

Social behaviour – social relationships

(a) Briefly explain what is meant by investment in Rusbult's theory of relationships. 2

(b) Explain what is meant by social exchange. 4

> Scott and Faye have been married for five years. They first got to know each other through chatting via an online wargame.

(c) Explain the hyperpersonal theory of relationships, with reference to the above scenario. 6

(d) Analyse a research study that investigated a theory of romantic relationships. 8

Question 8

Social behaviour – aggression

(a) Briefly explain what is meant by cognitive priming. 2

(b) Explain ethological influences on aggression. 4

> Leroy and his adoptive brother Kris are both high-achieving psychology students. However, Leroy is very calm and mild-mannered, while Kris tends to have angry outbursts. He finds his flatmates very irritating, and also tends to shout and swear at other road users when driving.

(c) Explain genetic influences on aggression, with reference to the above scenario. 6

(d) Analyse a research study that investigated media influences on aggression. 8

Practice exam 3

Duration – 2 hours 40 minutes

SECTION 1 – INDIVIDUAL BEHAVIOUR – 40 marks

Attempt Question 1 and ONE other from Questions 2, 3 or 4

Question 1

Individual behaviour – sleep and dreams   *Marks*

(a) Briefly explain what is meant by non-REM sleep.   2

(b) Explain how defence mechanisms could affect a person's dreams, according to
     the psychodynamic explanation of dreams.   6

> Lachlan is a student who is struggling to remember all of the information
> needed for his Psychology degree course. He is staying up late to study
> through the night. His classmate tells him that this is a bad idea, because sleep
> plays a role in information processing and consolidating new memories.

(c) Explain one or more cognitive processes relating to sleep and dreams, with reference to the
     scenario above.   4

(d) Analyse the findings of Dement and Kleitman's (1957) study of sleep.   8

Individual behaviour – optional topic

Attempt **EITHER**

Question 2 – depression

OR

Question 3 – memory

OR

Question 4 – stress

Question 2

Individual behaviour – depression

(a) Explain the role of hormones in depression.   4

> Dr Ahmed is speaking to one of her patients, a man in his 30s. She is concerned
> that his SRRI antidepressants are not working. She changes his prescription, and
> prescribes him a course of MAOI antidepressants instead.

(b) Analyse the use of SRRI and MAOI antidepressants, with reference to the
     scenario above.   8

(c) In Beck's cognitive theory of depression, explain what is meant by:

    i) Negative self-schemas.   4

    ii) Faulty information processing.   4

[Now go to Question 5]

Question 3

Individual behaviour – memory

(a) Explain the role of the sensory register in memory.   4

> Dr Chi is an educational psychologist. He is conducting a research study into
> how people learn about types of insect. To do so, he uses a computer program
> that shows images of insects one at a time. He has noticed that it is valuable for
> people to compare visual images of the creatures in his research, identifying
> the key differences between them. It also seems to be beneficial for them to
> hold the visual examples in mind for a few seconds, switching back and forth
> between them on the screen.

(b) Analyse the roles of the visuo-spatial sketchpad and central executive, with reference to the
     scenario above.   8

(c) In psychological explanations of forgetting, explain the role of:

    i) Context cues.   4

    ii) State cues.   4

[Now go to Question 5]

Question 4

Individual behaviour – stress

(a) Explain what is meant by hardiness. 4

> Mackenzie is a 5th year school pupil who has been studying for her Higher
> Maths exam for the last three weeks. As time has gone on, she has suffered
> from numerous minor health issues, such as mouth ulcers, a sore throat, and
> aches in her body.

(b) Analyse the role of stress in immunosuppression, with reference to the above scenario. 8

(c) In relation to sources of stress, explain the role of:

  i) Life changes. 4

  ii) Daily hassles. 4

[Now go to Question 5]

SECTION 2 – SOCIAL BEHAVIOUR – 40 marks

Attempt Question 5 and ONE other from Questions 6, 7 or 8

Question 5

Social behaviour – conformity and obedience   *Marks*

(a) Briefly explain one cultural factor that can affect conformity.   2

(b) Some studies into conformity and obedience have used observation. Explain the features
of the observation method.   4

(c) Analyse factors that affect obedience, with reference to research evidence.   14

Social behaviour – optional topic

Attempt **EITHER**

Question 6 – prejudice

OR

Question 7 – social relationships

OR

Question 8 – aggression

Question 6

Social behaviour – prejudice

> Lauren is a primary school pupil. Her class are currently watching a TV series about a group of children who travel through time to visit important events in history. Lauren asks why none of the children in the programme are black, and her teacher says he is not sure.

(a) Explain the media's ability to challenge stereotypes, with reference to the above scenario.   5

(b) Analyse social identity theory.   15

Question 7

Social behaviour – social relationships

> Paige is a disabled woman who works from home as a journalist. She's single, and lacks confidence in meeting new people.

(a) Explain the role of gating in virtual relationships, with reference to the above scenario.   5

(b) Analyse the evolutionary theory of relationships.   15

Question 8

Social behaviour – aggression

> Gary is a travel journalist who has been spending a lot of time in cities around Europe. He notices that at night, strangers are much more likely to act aggressively.

(a) Explain the role of disinhibition in aggression, with reference to the above scenario.   5

(b) Analyse social learning theory.   15

References

Abrams, D., & Houston, D. M. (2006). Equality, diversity and prejudice in Britain: results from the 2005 national survey. *Report for the Cabinet Office Equalities Review*. Kent: University of Kent Centre for the Study of Group Processes.

Abrams, D., Wetherell, M., Cochrane, S., Hogg, M. A., & Turner, J. C. (1990). Knowing what to think by knowing who you are: self-categorisation and the nature of norm formation. *British Journal of Social Psychology, 29*, 97–119.

Abramson, L. Y., Alloy, L. B., & Metalsky, G. I. (1988). The cognitive diathesis-stress theories of depression: Toward an adequate evaluation of the theories' validities. In L. B. Alloy (Ed.), *Cognitive processes in depression* (pp. 3–30). New York, NY, US: Guilford Press.

Adam, K., & Oswald, I. A. N. (1983). Protein synthesis, bodily renewal and the sleep-wake cycle. *Clinical Science, 65*(6), 561–567.

Adorno, T. W., Frenkel-Brunswik, E., Levinson, D. J., & Sanford, R. N. (1950). *The authoritarian personality*. New York: Harper.

Ainsworth, M. D. S., Bell, S. M., & Stayton, D. J. (1971). Individual differences in the strange-situation behaviour of one-year-olds. In H. R. Schaffer (Ed.), *The origins of human social relations* (pp. 17–52). New York: Academic Press.

Alloy, L. B., Reilly-Harrington, N., Fresco, D. M., Whitehouse, W. G., & Zechmeister, J. S. (1999). Cognitive styles and life events in subsyndromal unipolar and bipolar disorders: Stability and prospective prediction of depressive and hypomanic mood swings. *Journal of Cognitive Psychotherapy, 13*(1), 21–40.

Allport, G. (1954). *The nature of prejudice*. New York: Double-Day Anchor.

Altemeyer, B. (2006). *The authoritarians*. Retrieved 17 September 2018 from http://home.cc.umanitoba.ca/~altemey/

Ambady, N., Shih, M., Kim, A., & Pittinsky, T. L. (2001). Stereotype susceptibility in children: Effects of identity activation on quantitive performance. *Psychological Science, 12*(5), 385–390.

Anderson, C. A., & Dill, K. E. (2000). Video games and aggressive thoughts, feelings, and behavior in the laboratory and in life. *Journal of Personality and Social Psychology, 78*(4), 772–790.

Aronson, E., & Bridgeman, D. (1979). Jigsaw groups and the desegregated classroom: In pursuit of common goals. *Personality and Social Psychology Bulletin, 5*(4), 438–446.

Asch, S.E. (1951). Effects of group pressure upon the modification and distortion of judgment. In H. Guetzkow (Ed.), *Groups, leadership and men (pp. 222–236)*. Pittsburgh, PA: Carnegie Press.

Atkinson, R. C., & Shiffrin, R. M. (1968). Human memory: A proposed system and its control processes. In K.W. Spence and J.T. Spence (Eds.) *The psychology of learning and motivation*, Vol. 2 (pp. 89–195). London: Academic Press.

Baddeley, A. D. (1966). Short term memory for word sequences as a function of acoustic, semantic and formal similarity. *Quarterly Journal of Experimental Psychology, 18*, 362–5.

Baddeley, A. D. (2000). The episodic buffer: a new component of working memory? *Trends in Cognitive Sciences, 4*(11), 417–423.

Baddeley, A. D. and Hitch, G. (1974). Working memory. In G.H. Bower (Ed.), *The psychology of learning and motivation*, Vol 8 (pp. 47–89). London: Academic Press.

Baddeley, A. D., & Hitch, G. (1977). Recency re-examined. In S. Dornic (Ed.), *Attention and performance VI* (pp. 647–667). Hillsdale, NJ: Lawrence Erlbaum Associates.

Baddeley, A.D., Grant, W., Wight, E., & Thomson, N. (1975). Imagery and visual working memory. In P.M.A. Rabbitt & S. Dornic (Eds.), *Attention and performance V* (pp.205–217). London: Academic Press.

Baddeley, A. D., Thomson, N, & Buchanan, M. (1975). Word length and the structure of short-term memory. *Journal of Verbal Learning and Verbal Behaviour, 14*(6), 575–589.

Bandura, A., Ross, D., & Ross, S. A. (1963). Imitation of film-mediated aggressive models. *Journal of Abnormal and Social Psychology, 66*(1), 3–11.

Beck, A. (1976). *Cognitive therapy and the emotional disorders*. New York: International Universities Press.

Berscheid, E., Dion, K., Walster, E., & Walster, G. W. (1971). Physical attractiveness and dating choice: A test of the matching hypothesis. *Journal of Experimental Social Psychology, 7*(2), 173–189.

Bickman, L. (1974). Clothes make the person. *Psychology Today, 8*(4), 48–51.

Bjork, R. A. (1994). Memory and metamemory considerations in the training of human beings. In J. Metcalfe and A. Shimamura (Eds), *Metacognition: Knowing about knowing* (pp. 185–205). Cambridge, MA: MIT Press.

Brewer, M. B. (1968). Determinants of social distance among East African tribal groups. *Journal of Personality and Social Psychology, 10*(3), 279–289.

Brewer, M. B. (1988). A dual process model of impression formation. In T. K. Srul & R. S. Wyer (Eds), *Advances in social cognition. A dual process model of impression formation* (pp. 1–36). Hillsdale, NJ: Lawrence Erlbaum Associates.

Brown, G. L., Goodwin, F. K., Ballenger, J. C., Goyer, P.F., Major L. F. (1979). Aggression in humans correlates with cerebrospinal fluid amine metabolites. *Psychiatry Research, 1*(2), 131–139.

Brown, R. P., Charnsangavej, T., Keough, K. A., Newman, M. L., & Rentfrow, P. J. (2000). Putting the" affirm" into affirmative action: Preferential selection and academic performance. *Journal of Personality and Social Psychology, 79*(5), 736.

Bushman, B. J. (1998). Priming effects of media violence on the accessibility of aggressive constructs in memory. *Personality and Social Psychology Bulletin, 24*(5), 537–545.

Calhoun, J. B. (1962). Population density and social pathology. *Scientific American, 206*(3), 139–148.

Caspi, A., McClay, J., Moffitt, T. E., Mill, J., Martin, J., Craig, I. W., & Poulton, R. (2002). Role of genotype in the cycle of violence in maltreated children. *Science, 297*(5582), 851–854.

Chang, A. M., Aeschbach, D., Duffy, J. F., & Czeisler, C. A. (2015). Evening use of light-emitting eReaders negatively affects sleep, circadian timing, and next-morning alertness. *Proceedings of the National Academy of Sciences, 112*(4), 1232–1237.

Charlton, T. (1998). Reproaching television for violence in society: Passing the buck? Interim results from a naturalistic study in St Helena, South Atlantic. *Journal of Clinical Forensic Medicine, 5*(4), 169–171.

Craik, F. I. M., & Tulving, E. (1975). Depth of processing and the retention of words in episodic memory. *Journal of Experimental Psychology: General, 104*(3), 268–294.

Crick, F., & Mitchison, G. (1986). REM sleep and neural nets. *Journal of Mind and Behavior, 7*(2–3), 229–249.

Czeisler, C., Johnson, M. P., Duffy, J. F., Brown, E. N., Ronda, J. M., & Kronauer, R. E. (1990). Exposure to bright light and darkness to treat physiologic maladaption to night work. *New England Journal of Medicine, 322*, 1253–9.

DeLongis, A., Coyne, J. C., Dakof, G., Folkman, S., & Lazarus, R. S. (1982). The impact of daily hassles, uplifts and major life events to health status. *Health Psychology, 1*(2), 119–136.

Dement, W., & Kleitman, N. (1957). The relation of eye movements during sleep to dream activity: An objective method for the study of dreaming. *Journal of Experimental Psychology, 53*, 339–46.

Deutsch, M., & Gerrard, H. B. (1955). A study of normative and informational influence upon individual judgement. *Journal of Abnormal and Social Psychology, 51*, 629–36.

Dollard, J., Miller, N. E., Doob, L. W., Mowrer, O. H., & Sears, R. R. (1939). *Frustration and aggression*. New Haven, CT: Yale University Press.

Domhoff, G. W. (2005). The content of dreams: Methodologic and theoretical implications. In M.H. Kryger, T. Roth and W. C. Dement (Eds), *Principles and practices of sleep medicine*, 4th edn (pp. 522–534). Philadelphia: W.B. Saunders.

Duka, T., Weissenborn, R., & Dienes, Z. (2001). State-dependent effects of alcohol on recollective experience, familiarity and awareness of memories. *Psychopharmacology, 153*(3), 295–306.

Durkin, K., & Barber, B. (2002). Not so doomed: Computer game play and positive adolescent development. *Journal of Applied Developmental Psychology, 23*(4), 373–392.

Eagly, A. H. (1987). *Sex differences in social behaviour: A social-role interpretation*. Hillsdale, New Jersey: Lawrence Erlbaum.

Ekland-Olson, S., Barrick, D. M., & Cohen, L. E. (1983). Prison overcrowding and disciplinary problems: An analysis of the Texas prison system. *Journal of Applied Behavioral Science, 19*(2), 163–176.

Ferguson, C. J. (2014). Is video game violence bad? *The Psychologist, 27*(5), 324–327.

Folkman, S., Lazarus, R. S., Dunkel-Schetter, C., DeLongis, A., & Gruen, R. J. (1986). Dynamics of a stressful encounter: cognitive appraisal, coping, and encounter outcomes. *Journal of Personality and Social Psychology, 50*(5), 992–1003.

Freud, S. (1900/1991). The Interpretation of Dreams. In *The Complete Psychological Works of Sigmund Freud, Vol 4*. London: Penguin Books.

Freud, S. (1909/2002). Analysis of a phobia in a five year old boy. In *The 'Wolfman' and Other Cases* (Penguin Modern Classics). London: Penguin Books.

Friedman, M., & Rosenman, R. (1974). *Type A behavior and your heart*. New York: McGraw-Hill.

Fyock, J., & Stangor, C. (1994). The role of memory biases in stereotype maintenance. *British Journal of Social Psychology, 33*(3), 331–343.

Gathercole, S.E., & Baddeley, A. D. (1990) Phonological memory deficits in language disordered children: Is there a causal connection? *Journal of Memory and Language, 29*(3), 336–360.

Gergen, K. J., & Bauer, R. A. (1967). Interactive effects of self-esteem and task difficulty on social conformity. *Journal of Personality and Social Psychology, 6*(1), 16–22.

Giles, D. C., & Maltby, J. (2004). The role of media figures in adolescent development: Relations between autonomy, attachment, and interest in celebrities. *Personality and Individual Differences, 36*(4), 813–822.

Giles, D. C., & Maltby, J. (2006). Praying at the alter of the stars. *The Psychologist, 19*(5), 82–85.

Glanzer, M., & Cunitz, A. R. (1966). Two storage mechanisms in free recall. *Journal of Verbal Learning and Verbal Behaviour, 5*, 351–360.

Glick, P., & Fiske, S. T. (2001). An ambivalent alliance: Hostile and benevolent sexism as complementary justifications for gender inequality. *American Psychologist, 56*(2), 109–118.

Godden, D. R., & Baddeley, A. D. (1975). Context-dependent memory in two natural environments: On land and underwater. *British Journal of Psychology, 66*(3), 325–331.

Goldstein, D. S., & Kopin, I. J. (2007). Evolution of concepts of stress. *Stress, 10*(2), 109–120.

Gravel, J., Bouchard, M., Descormiers, K., Wong, J. S., & Morselli, C. (2013). Keeping promises: A systematic review and a new classification of gang control strategies. *Journal of Criminal Justice, 41*(4), 228–242.

Haney, C., Banks, W. C., & Zimbardo, P. G. (1973). A study of prisoners and guards in a simulated prison. *Naval Research Reviews, 9*, 1–17.

Harlow, H. F. (1959). Love in infant monkeys. *Scientific American, 200*(6), 688–74.

Harris, P. (2002). *Designing and reporting experiments in psychology* (2nd Ed). Maidenhead, Berkshire: Open University Press.

Hazan, C., & Shaver, P. R. (1987). Romantic love conceptualised as an attachment process. *Journal of Personality and Social Psychology, 52*(3), 511–524.

Hitch, G. J., & Baddeley, A. D. (1976). Verbal reasoning and working memory. *The Quarterly Journal of Experimental Psychology, 28*(4), 603–621.

Hobson, J. A. (2005). Sleep is of the brain, by the brain and for the brain. *Nature, 437*(7063), 1254–1256.

Hofling, C. K., Brotzman, E., Dalrymple, S., Graves, N., & Pierce, C. M. (1966). An experimental study in nurse-physician relationships. *Journal of Nervous and Mental Disease, 143*, 171–180.

Horne, J. A., & Harley, L. J. (1988). Human SWS following selective head heating during wakefulness. In: J.A. Horne (Ed.), *Sleep '88* (pp. 188–190). Stuttgart: Fischer Verlag.

Hornsey, M. J., Spears, R., Cremers, I., & Hogg, M. A. (2003). Relations between high and low power groups: the importance of legitimacy. *Personality and Social Psychology Bulletin, 29*, 216–227.

Irwin, J., & Cressey, D. R. (1962). Thieves, convicts and the inmate culture. *Social Problems, 10*(2), 142–155.

Jenness, A. (1932). The role of discussion in changing opinion regarding matter of fact. *Journal of Abnormal and Social Psychology, 27*, 279–296.

Judd, C. M., & Park, B. (1988). Out-group homogeneity: Judgments of variability at the individual and group levels. *Journal of Personality and Social Psychology, 54*(5), 778–788.

Jung, C. G. (1964). *Man and his symbols*. New York: Dell.

Kerckhoff, A. C., & Davis, K. E. (1962). Value consensus and need complementarity in mate selection. *American Sociological Review, 27*, 295–303.

Kiecolt-Glaser, J. K., Garner, W., Speicher, C. E., Penn, G. M., Holliday, J., & Glaser, R. (1984). Psychosocial modifiers of immunocompetence in medical students. *Psychosomatic Medicine, 46*, 7–14.

Kim, J., & Lee, J. E. R. (2011). The Facebook paths to happiness: Effects of the number of Facebook friends and self-presentation on subjective well-being. *CyberPsychology, Behavior, and Social Networking, 14*(6), 359–364.

Kobasa, S. C. (1979). Stressful life events, personality, and health: an inquiry into hardiness. *Journal of Personality and Social Psychology, 37*(1), 1–11.

Koriat, A., Bjork, R. A., Sheffer, L., & Bar, S. K. (2004). Predicting one's own forgetting: the role of experience-based and theory-based processes. *Journal of Experimental Psychology: General, 133*(4), 643.

Laar, C. V., Levin, S., Sinclair, S., & Sidanius, J. (2005). The effect of university roommate contact on ethnic attitudes and behaviour. *Journal of Experimental and Social Psychology, 41*, 329–345.

March, J. S., Silva, S., Petrycki, S., Curry, J., Wells, K., Fairbank, J., Burns, B., Domino, M., McNulty, S., Vitiello, B., & Severe, J. (2007). The treatment for adolescents with depression study (TADS): long-term effectiveness and safety outcomes. *Archives of General Psychiatry, 64*, 1132–43.

Marmot, M. G., Bosma, H., Hemingway, H., Brunner, E., & Stansfeld, S. (1997). Contribution of job control and other risk factors to social variations in coronary heart disease incidence. *Lancet, 350*(9073), 235–239.

Mazza, S., Gerbier, E., Gustin, M. P., Kasikci, Z., Koenig, O., Toppino, T. C., & Magnin, M. (2016). Relearn faster and retain longer: Along with practice, sleep makes perfect. *Psychological Science, 27*(10), 1321–1330.

McCutcheon, L. E., Lange, R., & Houran, J. (2002). Conceptualization and measurement of celebrity worship. *British Journal of Psychology, 93*(1), 67–87.

McGuffin, P., Katz, R., Rutherford, J., & Watkins, S. (1996). The heritability of DSM-IV unipolar depression: a hospital based twin register study. *Archives of General Psychiatry, 53*, 129–136.

Mednick, S., Nakayama, K., & Stickgold, R. (2003). Sleep-dependent learning: a nap is as good as a night. *Nature Neuroscience, 6*(7), 697–698.

Meichenbaum, D. (2007). Stress inoculation training: A preventative and treatment approach. In Lehrer, P.M., Woolfolk, R.L. and Sime, W.E. (Eds), *Principles and practice of stress management* , 3rd edn (pp. 497–518.). New York: Guilford Press.

Milgram, S. (1963). Behavioural study of obedience. *Journal of Abnormal and Social Psychology, 67*, 371–8.

Milgram, S. (1974). *Obedience to authority*. New York: Harper and Row.

Mori, K., & Arai, M. (2010). No need to fake it: Reproduction of the Asch experiment without confederates. *International Journal of Psychology, 45*(5), 390–397.

Murdock Jr, B. B. (1962). The serial position effect of free recall. *Journal of Experimental Psychology, 64*(5), 482.

Murstein, B. I. (1972). Physical attractiveness and marital choice. *Journal of Personality and Social Psychology, 22*(1), 8–12.

Nuckolls, K. B., Cassel, J., & Kaplan, B. H. (1972). Psychological Assets, life crisis and the prognosis of pregnancy. *American Journal of Epidemiology, 95*, 431–441.

Oswald, I. (1966). *Sleep*. London: Penguin.

Paluck, E. L. (2009). Reducing intergroup prejudice and conflict using the media: A field experiment in Rwanda. *Journal of Personality and Social Psychology, 96*(3), 574–587.

Perrin, S., & Spencer, C. (1981). Independence or conformity in the Asch experiment as a reflection of cultural and situational factors. *British Journal of Social Psychology, 20*(3), 205–209.

Peterson, L. R., & Peterson, M. J. (1959). Short-term retention of individual verbal items. *Journal of Experimental Psychology, 58*, 193–198.

Pettigrew, T. F., & Martin, J. (1987). Shaping the organizational context for Black American inclusion. *Journal of Social Issues, 43*(1), 41–78.

Rahe, R.H., Mahan, J., & Arthur, R. (1970). Predictions of near-future health-change from subjects' preceding life changes. *Journal of Psychosomatic Research, 14*, 401–406.

Raine, A., Buchsbaum, M., & LaCasse, L. (1997). Brain abnormalities in murderers indicated by positron emission tomography. *Biological Psychiatry, 42*(6), 495–508.

Rasch, B., & Born, J. (2013). About sleep's role in memory. *Physiological Review, 93*, 681–766.

Read, J., & Arnold, C. (2017). Is electroconvulsive therapy for depression more effective than placebo? A systematic review of studies since 2009. *Ethical Human Psychology and Psychiatry, 19*(1), 5–23.

Riggle, E. D., Ellis, A. L., & Crawford, A. M. (1996). The impact of "media contact" on attitudes toward gay men. *Journal of Homosexuality, 31*(3), 55–69.

Roediger III, H. L., & Karpicke, J. D. (2006). Test-enhanced learning: Taking memory tests improves long-term retention. *Psychological Science, 17*(3), 249–255.

Rotter, J. B. (1966). Generalized expectancies for internal versus external control of reinforcement. *Psychological Monographs, 80* (Whole No. 609).

Rusbult, C. E. (1980). Commitment and satisfaction in romantic associations: A test of the investment model. *Journal of Experimental Social Psychology, 16*(2), 172–186.

Rusbult, C. E., & Martz, J. M. (1995). Remaining in an abusive relationship: An investment model analysis of nonvoluntary dependence. *Personality and Social Psychology Bulletin, 21*(6), 558–571.

Rutland, A. (1999). The development of national prejudice, in-group favouritism and self-stereotypes in British children. *British Journal of Social Psychology, 38*, 55–70.

Sapolsky, R. M. (1995). Social subordinance as a marker of hypercortisolism: Some unexpected subtleties. *Annals of the New York Academy of Sciences, 771*, 626–639.

Scoville, W. B., & Milner, B. (1957). Loss of recent memory after bilateral hippocampal lesions. *Journal of Neurology, Neurosurgery and Psychiatry, 20*, 11–21.

Selye, H. (1936). A syndrome produced by diverse nocuous agents. *Nature, 138*, 32.

Shapiro, C. M., Bortz, R., Mitchell, D., Bartel, P., & Jooste, P. (1981) Slow-wave sleep: a recovery period after exercise. *Science, 214*(4526), 1253–1254.

Sheridan, L., Maltby, J., & Gillett, R. (2006). Pathological public figure preoccupation: Its relationship with dissociation and absorption. *Personality and Individual Differences, 41*(3), 525–535.

Sherif, M., Harvey, O. J., White, B. J., Hood, W. R., & Sherif, C. W. (1954). *Experimental study of positive and negative intergroup attitudes between experimentally produced groups.* Oklahoma: University of Oklahoma Press.

Sproull, L., & Kiesler, S. (1986). Reducing social context cues: Electronic mail in organizational communication. *Management Science, 32*(11), 1492–1512.

Suler, J. R. (2002). Identity management in cyberspace. *Journal of Applied Psychoanalytic Studies, 4*(4), 455–459.

Suler, J. (2004). The online disinhibition effect. *Cyberpsychology & Behavior, 7*(3), 321–326.

Sykes, G. M. (1958). *The society of captives: A study of a maximum security prison.* New York: Princeton University Press.

Tajfel, H. (1970). Experiments in intergroup discrimination. *Scientific American, 223*, 96–105.

Tajfel, H., & Turner, J. C. (1979). An integrative theory of intergroup conflict. In: Austin, W.G. and Worchel, S. (Eds), *The social psychology of intergroup relations* (pp. 33–47). Monterey, CA: Brooks/Cole.

Thibaut, J. W., & Kelley, H. H. (1959). *The social psychology of groups*. New York: Wiley.

Tinbergen, N. (1952). The curious behavior of the stickleback. *Scientific American, 187*(6), 22–27.

Tosun, L. P., & Lajunen, T. (2010). Does Internet use reflect your personality? Relationship between Eysenck's personality dimensions and Internet use. *Computers in Human Behavior, 26*(2), 162–167.

Trivers, R.L. (1972). Parental investment and sexual selection. In B. Campbell (Ed.), *Sexual selection and the descent of man* (pp. 136–179). Chicago: Adeline.

Velez, J. A., Greitemeyer, T., Whitaker, J. L., Ewoldsen, D. R., & Bushman, B. J. (2016). Violent video games and reciprocity: The attenuating effects of cooperative game play on subsequent aggression. *Communication Research, 43*(4), 447–467.

Walther, J. B. (1996). Computer-mediated communication: Impersonal, interpersonal, and hyperpersonal interaction. *Communication Research, 23*(1), 3–43.

Walther, J. B., Kashian, N., Jang, J. W., Shin, S. Y., Dai, Y., & Koutamanis, M. (2018). The effect of message persistence and disclosure on liking in computer-mediated communication. *Media Psychology, 21*(2), 308–327.

Waugh, N. C., & Norman, D. A. (1965). Primary memory. *Psychological Review, 72*, 89–104.

Wedekind, C., Seebeck, T., Bettens, F., & Paepke, A. J. (1995). MHC-dependent mate preferences in humans. *Proceedings of the Royal Society of London. Series B: Biological Sciences, 260*(1359), 245–249.

Williams, T. M. (1986). *The impact of television: A natural experiment in three communities.* New York: Academic Press.

Wolfson, A. R., & Carskadon, M. A. (1998). Sleep schedules and daytime functioning in adolescents. *Child Development, 69*(4), 875–887.